12/21

the assassination

tAriq Ali

the assassination
WHO KILLED INDIRA G?

Seagull
BOOKS

london new york calcutta

Seagull Books

Editorial offices:

1st Floor, Angel Court, 81 St Clements Street,
Oxford OX4 1AW, UK

1 Washington Square Village, Apt 1U, New York,
NY 10012, USA

26 Circus Avenue, Calcutta 700 017, India

Seagull Books 2008

ISBN-13   978 1 9054 2 285 2

British Library Cataloguing-in-Publication Data
A catalogue record for this book is available from the British Library

Typeset by Seagull Books, Calcutta, India
Printed in the United Kingdom by Biddles Ltd, King's Lynn

CONTENTS

This was the first draft of a TV screenplay for Channel Four television, part of The Assassination Quartet which also included similar treatments of the assassinations of Zulfiqar Ali Bhutto, Sheikh Mujibur Rehman and Solomon Bandaranaike. All four leaders were killed and their deaths spawned dynasties that still dominate South Asian politics. I did not do any more work on this play when the project was scuppered and it is presented here unchanged.

Tariq Ali
London, June 2008

THE ASSASSINATION

Scene 1

EXTERIOR. A CROWDED STREET IN A SUBCONTINENTAL TOWN.

It is late afternoon in spring. There is a high level of noise pollution. Motorcycle, rickshaw and car noises mingle with the sound of permanently ringing cycle bells and honking lorries.

A dark blue jeep leaves a government building and the policeman on guard salutes the occupant. We track it as it joins the traffic and see the front-seat passenger in close-up— a senior police officer in uniform.

From a small side street, a motorcycle carrying two turbaned Sikhs emerges and unobtrusively joins the throng, maintaining a safe distance from the jeep.

As the traffic recedes, the jeep enters a tree-lined residential area, with old bungalows much in evidence. The jeep picks up speed. So does the motorcycle. We see the young Sikh faces in close-up.

The motorcycle reaches the jeep and is ready to overtake when the Sikh driver turns and looks at the cop—they are virtually face to face—and gives him a friendly wave. The policeman, pleasantly surprised, waves back and smiles. The bike edges forward and the policeman's smile turns to horror as he notices the other Sikh pointing a revolver at him. Before he can shout, he has been shot in the head and neck at point-blank range. The jeep lurches to a halt on the side of the road and the motorcyclists speed away.

3

Opening Credits

Police sirens and roadblocks. Sikhs being stopped and searched.

Scene 2

INTERIOR. A LARGE CONFERENCE ROOM IN A GOVERNMENT
BUILDING IN THE CAPITAL.

*The same afternoon. The room has been darkened. Images
are being projected on to a giant screen. Watching them are a
dozen blurred shapes, unrecognizable in the dark. One of the
images on the screen is fairly large. Suddenly, the images
change to the jerky style of clandestinely filmed home movies:
a man in a suit is getting into his car surrounded by several
armed bodyguards outside a large white building (large not
in height but in breadth). Before he gets into his car, he looks
around nervously and we get a very clear picture of his
fleshy, bespectacled face. He gets into the car and the car
drives off. In the next shot, we see the same man at a reception with a General and a Western diplomat. Freeze frame on
the triumvirate.*

MALE VOICE. The three rogues together, Madame! (*We
focus on each face as he gives their rank*) The mad sci-
entist is flanked by their head of Inter-Services
Intelligence and the CIA Station Chief.

The screen goes blank and the room is totally dark.

FEMALE VOICE. So what?

*Silence, as the blinds are pulled back and light floods into the
room. It is a very select gathering. The Prime Minister is seated*

on a sofa at the very front of the screen. She is dressed in a khaki-brown sari, indicating the military character of the occasion. She is accompanied by her Defence Minister and Intelligence chief. There is a further silence as they wait for her to speak.

PRIME MINISTER. I thought you had new material. This is all old stuff. The whole world knows about the nuclear reactor and the madman who runs it. So you have a picture of him with one of their Generals and John Benson of the CIA. (*Shrugs her shoulders*) Anything more concrete? Have you any real evidence of what they're up to?

Two Generals appear perplexed but the third smiles in agreement.

GENERAL SINGH. Madame, we have proof. Secret documents in which the Generals boast that they're only a screwdriver away from the bomb. Washington knows that very well. (*Hands her a file marked 'Top Secret: For Prime Minister Only'*) When you read my report, you'll see that our choices are limited. If you could read the file, Madame, we would like another meeting. Tonight, if possible.

She ignores the last request and rises, smiling. All rise to their feet and Generals stand to attention. She walks to the exit. All follow.

GENERAL SINGH (*pleading, just as she reaches the door*). Madame?

6

PRIME MINISTER (*stopping*). I know, I know. You want a
   meeting. Urgent? (*Two Generals nod.*) Tomorrow
   morning at 8. My office. (*Smiles and walks out.*)
All follow.

Scene 3

EXTERIOR. OUTSIDE GOVERNMENT BUILDING. A NUMBER OF
CARS ARE PARKED WITH CHAUFFEURS ON THE READY.

*As PM and party walk out of the doors, the chauffeurs stiffen
and extinguish their cigarettes. PM is followed by an armed
Sikh bodyguard who opens the door of her car. Generals
salute farewell and she nods and gets into the car. The bodyguard gets into the front. A jeep full of uniformed and armed
police prepare to follow the car. It is now dusk and, as the car
drives off followed by the jeep, the city lights are switched on.*

Scene 4

INTERIOR. CAR DRIVING SHORT DISTANCE TO PM'S RESIDENCE.

We observe PM studying the preamble of the document in the file.

GENERAL SINGH (*voiceover*). The political repercussions of what we propose, either in this region or globally, are not the concern of this document. That is for you and the Cabinet to determine before you take any decisions. Given the gravity of the crisis, however, we would recommend that the whole Cabinet is not informed at this stage. (*PM smiles and flicks through the other sheets till her eyes are arrested by a paragraph.*) The successful pre-emptive Israeli raid on the Iraqi nuclear reactor is a useful model in this regard. For the success of Operation Baghdad a strike is necessary this year, before Washington and the West give the Generals too many sophisticated weapons. (*PM closes the folder slowly but clutches it tightly. She shuts her eyes.*)

PM (*voiceover, to herself*). Another war.

Scene 5

EXTERIOR. DRIVE AND FRONT OF PM'S RESIDENCE.

A palatial colonial bungalow with large lawns at front and back. It is almost dark and the lights are on in the porch as the car drives in. The jeep stops just outside the front gates. The Sikh bodyguard opens the door for her and salutes. Her grandchildren—a teenage girl and boy—rush out of the front door to welcome her back.

GRANDDAUGHTER. You're very late. The guests have
     been waiting for ages.

PM rushes inside.

Scene 6

INTERIOR. FRONT HALL. PM'S RESIDENCE.

As she enters, there is a flurry of activity. Servants rush in to receive orders. Her PA hovers respectfully, waiting for instructions. He offers to take the file but she keeps it with her.

PM (*to granddaughter*). Tell them I'm here. I'll only be a minute. Just going to wash. Tell the kitchen to get dinner ready immediately. (*Walks into a side room in a corridor.*)

Scene 7

INTERIOR. LIVING ROOM. PM'S RESIDENCE.

A tastefully decorated room without being too ornate. Lots of family photographs. A famous actor and a famous novelist (Peter Ustinov and Barbara Cartland) are waiting patiently with glasses in their hands. Talking to them is PM's daughter-in-law, suitably attired in a sari despite her European antecedents. PM walks in. All rise. She hugs the novelist who shrieks with delight .

NOVELIST. My dear! How nice. Long, long, time! How well you look!

PM (*smiling*). Forgive the sari—I know how much you hate brown (*more laughter and shrieks*) but there was no time to change. (*Shakes hands warmly with the actor*) Lovely to see you. I so enjoyed seeing you as Puck!

Laughter. Servant enters and whispers in her ear and she rises

PM. Come, you've waited too long already. Dinner is served. (*Takes famous actor's arm and escorts him out of the room.*)

Others follow.

Scene 8

INTERIOR. DINING ROOM. US AMBASSADOR'S RESIDENCE.

Ambassador and his wife are entertaining a few guests at a small dinner party. The atmosphere is informal even though Ambassador and his wife are formally dressed. The six guests are less so.

AMBASSADOR'S WIFE. Then I told him I'd buy the statue for five thousand dollars. No more. And he agreed. Just wanted it there and then. (*All laugh.*)

AMBASSADOR. Back on the West Coast, this lady is deeply hostile. I repeat, deeply hostile to my business interests. Here she bargains like a street pedlar to buy antiques cheap and take them out of this poor country illegally. I don't know what it is but her repressed free enterprise instincts have come straight out into the open! (*Laughter. Smartly dressed servant enters and whispers in Ambassador's ear.*) Excuse me, I must take a call. (*He walks to the sideboard and picks up a telephone. Others try and carry on talking but keep an ear open to his conversation.*) Hi there, Chuck! (*Longish silence as his face grows tense*) Yes, yes . . . I understand. OK, give me half an hour. (*Puts the phone down and is very thoughtful.*)

AMBASSADOR'S WIFE. What does he want now? Can't it
wait till the morning?

AMBASSADOR. No. Chuck says it can't and he never pan-
ics. And I don't know what it's about. I'm sorry
everyone. I'll be back soon. Don't run away. The
house is yours.

Scene 9

INTERIOR. DINING ROOM. PM'S RESIDENCE.

An informal family dinner is in progress with the two guests. Ustinov has just finished doing an imitation of a US president and everyone around the table—including PM—is laughing.

PM. But we're not the world's largest democracy for nothing. Actors started entering politics in our provinces long before in the United States. So there's a bigger future for you here, Mr Ustinov.

CARTLAND. My dear, is it true that one of these actors— you know, the one who's a chief minister of some state—the one who defeated your party (*PM nods*)—is it true that he's a transvestite?

PM. Only at night. (*Laughter*) I am told he wears a sari when he goes to sleep. You know, in our religion every Hindu has the attributes of a man and a woman. In his case I think it's 60:40.

More laughter.

USTINOV. Before I forget Madame, I'm here for a special reason. (*She looks at him*) I'm making a documentary on the old trade routes in India and I'd like to interview you at the beginning. Possible?

PM. Of course. No problem. (*As servants remove plates and begin to clear the table for the next course, one of them whispers something in her ear.*) Excuse me for a moment. (*Leaves.*)

Scene 10

INTERIOR. PM'S SMALL OFFICE/STUDY AT HOME.

PA is waiting in the room as she storms in.

PM. What is it? Couldn't it wait?

PA. It's bad news, Madame. The Inspector General of Police in Punjab has been shot dead by terrorists.

PM (*her face paling*). When? Why wasn't I told before? Why is security so bad?

PA. I was informed a few minutes ago. It happened when you were with the military.

PM. Ring General Singh. Tell him the meeting is on for tonight. Tell them to come here (*looking at her watch*) in one hour's time. Is that clear? (*PA nods*) And find them, wherever they are . . .

Scene 11

EXTERIOR. US EMBASSY.

A large impressive modern building with the Stars and Stripes flying day and night. The building is well lit and heavily guarded. Ambassador's car drives to the front. His Indian chauffeur leaps out and opens the door. Ambassador, a sprightly 67, runs up the stairs.

Scene 12

INTERIOR. AMBASSADOR'S OFFICE. US EMBASSY.

Ambassador and Charles Davis, CIA Station Chief, are pouring out drinks. As they sit, Davis hands Ambassador a sheaf of papers in a file marked 'Security: Operation Baghdad'.

CHUCK. When you read these you'll see why I dragged you here at this hour. It's serious. They're planning an Israeli-type raid on the nuclear reactor next door. The Prime Minister is meeting with her Generals to discuss their proposals further. Given that she's losing popularity at home, she might be tempted. If they go in, it could risk our entire strategy in the region. I suggest you see her tomorrow and let her know that we know and we disapprove. I'd like to fly to Washington the day after and discuss the matter further. It could get serious, Mr Ambassador. Very, very serious.

AMBASSADOR. Hold on a minute, Chuck. Are you sure it isn't a game plan? After all, our top brass has hundreds of game plans and computer war strategies. Are you one hundred per cent certain that this is for real?

CHUCK. I'm convinced that the Army High Command is serious. What is uncertain is whether she'll back them. We might not like to believe this, but in this country an elected prime minister has more authority over the Armed Forces than the President in the United States. (*Smiles patronizingly.*)

AMBASSADOR. OK Chuck. I'll see her tomorrow if she'll see me. You know what she's like. The last time it took me 10 whole days.

CHUCK. I think she'll see you.

Scene 13

INTERIOR. PM'S OFFICE/STUDY AT HOME.

PM is seated on a comfortable armchair. Two of the Generals we have seen before are seated on a sofa. She is still in her khaki-brown sari, but the men are out of uniform.

PM. Are you sure we can win quickly? If I were to agree—and I say IF—how long would it take?

GENERAL SINGH. Half a day at most, Madame.

She looks at the other General.

GENERAL SHARMA. Perhaps a day, but no longer.

She stares at them for a while, finding it difficult to believe that they can be so obtuse.

PM. I am astonished at how naïve both of you are. Operation Baghdad is nonsense. The Israelis could do it in a day because the Americans were backing them and the Russians, as we know too well, never intervene. So Israel has a great deal to gain and nothing to lose. We have a lot to lose and very little to gain. The situation is almost reversed. The entire Western bloc is backing them because of Afghanistan. Washington, as you know only fights for democracy in Eastern Europe. Not even China! (*Generals laugh*) And even in Europe they

21

don't mind military dictators. Look at Greece and
Turkey. If our country was half the size, I think you
two would be in power and I would be in prison.
(*Generals laugh and mutter disclaimers. She smiles.*) Do
you understand what I'm saying? In a world of
double standards, we cannot do what Israel did to
Iraq. Operation Baghdad is a non-starter.

GENERAL SHARMA. The Americans didn't like it when we
liberated Bangladesh, Madame. They huffed and
puffed and talked about the Seventh Fleet and tilt-
ing towards the military next door, but they were
impotent. Even magazines hostile to us called you
the Empress of India.

She smiles.

GENERAL SINGH. It was all bluff. The Vietnamese were
giving them a bloody nose in Indo-China. Their
own people were against more interventions.

PM. Yes, yes, yes. But most importantly there was a
mass revolt in East Bengal. That's why WE won!
Not that it did us much good. The Americans had
poor Mujib bumped off. Replaced him with tried
and tested collaborators. They've got that country
too now. In their pocket. The situation's different
now anyway. (*Generals look demoralized. There is
silence as she watches them. Then, suddenly, her mood
changes.*) You see, what is involved is something

22

much, much bigger. Forget Baghdad. Concentrate on the Falklands option.

GENERAL SINGH (*surprised*). Madame!?

PM (*her mood now no longer reflective but iron ladyish*). Think carefully. There's more to our neighbour than the threat of a bomb. They're arming and funding the Sikh extremists. Your own intelligence reports indicate that they have set up several training camps. (*Angry*) My Inspector General of Police was gunned down this afternoon. By men we'll never find because they've crossed the border. The Golden Temple's become a den of murderers. That Sikh Rasputin issues daily orders to kill other Sikhs and Hindus. Our options are limited. You two want a one-day raid on their nuclear reactor. Even if we succeed, it could mobilize their nationalism. More importantly, the strength of their army would be unaffected. (*Pause*) We will destroy the reactor, but with a fully-fledged plan to topple the dictator and pave the way for a return to democracy. The only time we've had peace is when a civilian's run their country. You're shocked?!

GENERAL SHARMA. Madame, you've taken us unawares. We have to think hard.

PM. Of course! As long as it's a bombing raid carried out by our Air Force, you don't think hard enough! But now that I'm suggesting an operation that involves ground troops, you get worried? Aren't you up to it, General?

GENERAL SINGH. No, no, Madame. Don't misunderstand us. It's just that the logistics of what you propose are totally different.

PM (*smiling*). When we're planning a shoot, it's much better to kill the beast rather than wound it. Is it not? (*Both men look at each other, laugh and look at her admiringly*) Think about the Falklands option seriously. I want to see a plan by next week. (*She smiles and they realize the interview is over. Both men stand up to attention and leave. She begins scribbling some notes on a piece of paper.*)

Scene 14

EXTERIOR. A SPECIAL MILITARY TRAINING CAMP IN A NEIGH-
BOURING COUNTRY NOT FAR FROM THE INDIAN BORDER.

*We view the camp, which is relatively small, and see two or
three men being trained in different forms of terrorist activity—
detonating devices, throwing grenades, firing at moving targets from motorcycles, target practice with revolvers and moving targets, physical training. We cut in on a group of men
in khaki, but without any markings, who are viewing the
progress on the ground. Three of them are subcontinentals,
one is a black American. In a corner, two young Sikhs are
being shaved and shorn of their hair. They are clearly nervous and are talking to each other in Punjabi.*

YOUNG SIKH (*much more relaxed*). Yes, yes, brother. The
high priests gave us permission.

*A jeep drives into the camp. As it is sighted, activity stops.
Everyone rushes to the jeep, cheering, and, in their enthusiasm,
braving the dust clouds raised by it. The two assassins who
have killed the police chief step out of the jeep, pleased with the
adulation. They are embraced and hugged. The training officers walk up to them and they salute. Hands are shaken. Then
the two men walk to a tap and wash their faces. An attendant
comes up and takes off their beards, unwinds their turbans and
removes their wigs. We see them clean-shaven and smiling as
buckets of water are poured on them by the others.*

Scene 15

EXTERIOR. STREETS OF CAPITAL.

Ambassador's giant Lincoln with full regalia is being driven to PM's office. In the back of the car are Ambassador and Chuck.

AMBASSADOR. I'll warn her off, Chuck. But it's not easy. This is probably the only truly independent state in the Third World. Can't treat its leader as if she were one of our banana men.

CHUCK. Be respectful, Sir, but firm. She knows why you're coming. (*Ambassador looks at him*) Oh sure she knows. Why do you think she agreed to see you today?

Car drives in front of PM's office. Ambassador and Chuck alight and enter through the front of the building.

Scene 16

INTERIOR. ENTRANCE, STAIRS AND CORRIDORS. PM'S OFFICE.

The architecture (Lutyens) is rich, but the furnishings and decor are shabby. Ambassador signs in the book and is escorted upstairs by a uniformed peon. Not a word is said as he marches down the corridor. At the other end, PM's PA is waiting. He welcomes Ambassador and takes him to a modestly furnished anteroom.

PA. Please stay here for a few minutes. Tea or soft drinks?

Both men shake their heads.

We follow PA out of the room and into the corridor. He rushes to PM's room and knocks. Then enters. PM—dressed in a yellow sari—is sitting behind her desk, poring over a file. She does not look up. PA coughs. She looks up.

PA. The Ambassador is here, Madame. Should I show him in?

PM. Let him wait for 10 minutes. Then bring him in. (*Exit PA. She stands up and paces up and down. We hear her thoughts. 'I wonder how much they know. Sharma and Singh are safe, but not Lal. They might have got wind of Operation Baghdad. Can't be anything else.' She stands below her father's photograph and*

smiles at it. '*I know how you would have reacted. Angry,
imperious, dismissive. You always loathed the Americans,
didn't you? Couldn't hide it very well. I prefer their
bluntness to the over subtlety of your old English friends.*'
Smiles as knock sounds on door and returns to her desk.
Her face is stern again.) Come in. (*Ambassador enters.
She rises and offers him a limp hand. He shakes her hand
and half-bows. She escorts him to the other end of the room
where there is an ugly, hard sofa and two matching arm-
chairs. She takes a chair. He sits on the sofa. Tea is served.
She signals to PA to leave. They are alone.*)

AMBASSADOR. It was very kind of you to see me at such
short notice, Prime Minister.

PM (*smiling*). You said it was extremely urgent.

AMBASSADOR (*clearing his throat and fidgeting*). We have
received some disturbing information, er . . . er . . .
from Washington actually and I was asked to confirm or deny the reports. (*She stares at him sweetly as
she pours out some tea*) Er . . . er . . . it appears that
some hotheads in your military are in favour of
repeating the Israeli raid on Baghdad. Only this
time on the nuclear reactor next door.

PM. My dear Ambassador, where on earth did you get
that information? (*Laughs*) I hope somebody hasn't
been making a fool of you?

AMBASSADOR. So it's totally without foundation?

PM. Listen, Excellency. In your country you believe that
your security is permanently threatened by the
Soviet Union. You do believe that, don't you?

AMBASSADOR (*taken unawares*). Oh, yeah, yeah. Sure we
do!

PM. So if we found some discarded game plan showing
how you intended to get in a first strike and
destroy the Soviet Union's capacities and confront-
ed you with preparing a war, what would you say?
(*Ambassador smiles politely.*) The military everywhere
is paranoid. Anything else?

AMBASSADOR (*embarrassed*). I'm very relieved to hear
that Prime Minister. Very, very relieved. (*He is about
to get up, when she starts talking again. He is undecided
whether to sit down again or remain standing. She
solves his dilemma by rising slowly herself.*)

PM. One more thing. (*She starts walking him to the door.*)
We are deeply concerned at the arms build-up
next door. We are even more perturbed at their
nuclear plan and we note that your government is
arming them to the hilt. (*He starts to speak but she
stops him with a gesture*) I know. They're being
armed to fight the Russians in Afghanistan. Years
ago, it was the Chinese threat. But every time they
turned your guns at us. (*Cold*) Please convey my
concern to Washington. (*She offers him her hand. He*

shakes it and exits. She returns to her desk and sits, deep in thought. Her PA enters, but watches her without saying anything for a second or two.)

PA. Madame, there are three more people waiting, but er . . . er . . . there is a message from Parliament. (*She looks up impatiently*) The Defence Minister would like you to come and deal with the Opposition yourself. The latest killing has created pandemonium in the House and no one else can handle it.

PM. Cancel all appointments till tomorrow.

Scene 17

EXTERIOR. STREETS OF CAPITAL.

Ambassador's car driving back to the Embassy. Ambassador and Chuck talk as the car drives into the Embassy compound and US Marines salute the flag.

CHUCK. I tell you she's lying. The General who spoke to us was not talking about game plans.

AMBASSADOR. Are you sure, Chuck? It wouldn't be the first time your boys have been misinformed.

CHUCK (*angry*). Mr Ambassador, I know my fucking job. General Lal has been on our payroll since he was a Colonel in the military intelligence. All his information—I repeat ALL—has so far been one hundred per cent accurate. Why should he be wrong now?

AMBASSADOR. That's not my business. I tell you she convinced me. Operation Baghdad is a fake.

Scene 18

INTERIOR. PARLIAMENT IN SESSION.

All the benches are packed. The government ministers are tense. PM's seat is empty and it shows in the packed house. An Opposition MP is on his feet, speaking with passion.

OPPOSITION MP 1. The complicity of your government with the extremists is well known.

Shouts and denials from government backbenchers.

SPEAKER. Order, order. (*Noise subsides*) If this carries on, I will suspend the House for the day.

OPPOSITION MP 2. That's what they want. They're running scared.

Speaker glares at him. Silence. He nods at Opposition MP to continue speaking.

OPPOSITION MP 1. Mr Speaker, I must move that the House establishes a Commission of Enquiry to investigate these killings. Why are our security forces paralysed? Who is supplying the terrorists with arms and why? The Inspector General of Police is gunned down in cold blood by these saffron-turbaned loonies while their leader sits safely in the sanctuary of the Golden Temple and boasts of his successes to the Western media. I accuse (*pointing to the government benches*) them of

having encouraged this man in the hope that he
will marginalize their moderate opponents. Now
he's become a Frankenstein. Be warned! You have
nurtured a monster—he'll take you down with
him!

*Pandemonium as government MPs wave papers, throw paper
darts, scream angrily. Shouts of 'Withdraw these charges',
'We know you' to PM as she enters. Her supporters are
silenced by her presence. She walks modestly to her seat and
sits down.*

OPPOSITION MP 3. Her Majesty has arrived. Now we can
get some answers. Could the Prime Minister tell us
who killed the Inspector General?

PM (*on her feet*). The matter is being investigated.
(*Shouts of 'By whom? The men in the temple?'*) I am
convinced that the extremists are being funded
and armed by foreign powers. (*Silence*) We shall
report all our findings to this House. But please,
no more wild accusations. The security of our State
is at risk.

OPPOSITION MP 1. We realize that Prime Minister, but
could you tell us why the main inspirer of the
extremists secretly met your Home Minister six
months ago? What did they discuss?

HOME MINISTER (*a Sikh*). That is a lie. A total lie, Mr
Speaker!

OPPOSITION MP 1. I repeat, Mr Speaker, that the Home
　　　Minister met with the extremists to discuss plans to
　　　discredit the moderate Opposition party and
　　　destabilize the government. The plan misfired
　　　badly and now we're in a mess. (*Points his finger at
　　　PM*) And she is the architect of all this chaos. Her
　　　obsession with power at any price and at all costs
　　　has brought the country to this state.

*Pandemonium on government benches. PM smiles at
Opposition, but noise continues.*

SPEAKER (*rising to his feet*). I suspend this session for the
　　　rest of the day.

*Angry Opposition MPs shout as Speaker withdraws from
chamber followed by PM. MPs throw papers at each other as
the House disintegrates into chaos.*

Scene 19

INTERIOR. CABINET MEETING ROOM. GOVERNMENT BUILDING.

PM is sitting at the table. There are three other Cabinet Ministers present—Defence, Home and Foreign Affairs—all looking tense and drawn. Peons wheel in a large TV and VTR.

PM. This time he's gone too far.

The VTR is switched on and the TV screen is filled with archive material of the Golden Temple and the armed men who have occupied it. There are establishing shots.

TV (*voiceover*). Here in the holies, the Golden Temple, there are armed Sikhs who say that they are fighting for an independent homeland.

We see and hear the Sikh leader in the temple defending his policies and mocking PM and the government.

PM (*to Home Minister, with bitterness*). You said, 'Everything is under control.' This man is totally out of control. (*Stares at him.*)

HOME MINISTER. He took our money and demanded our protection. I thought he would play but he's gone wild, Madame. Only one way left.

PM (*angry*). You knew these people. Why couldn't you see this happening? Awful mess! (*To Defence Minister*) There's only one solution—they've got to be flushed out! Soon! It'll be messy but it must be swift. Talk to General Singh and prepare a plan. (*To Home Minister*) You'd better go now and see if this imbecile will give up without a fight. Offer him money, but get him out. (*Home Minister nods, but remains seated*) I suggest you leave now. I want a report by tomorrow. (*Home Minister rises and leaves*) Well, what do you think of Operation Baghdad.

FOREIGN SECRETARY. Very risky, Madame. The Americans—

PM. Already know. The Ambassador called this morning. (*Ministers look shocked*) They've got their informers in the High Command. Nothing new. I denied it, but . . .

DEFENCE MINISTER. It has the advantage of being a one-day affair. Minimum losses, maximum advantage.

PM. Yes, yes, that's the Army line, but its unrealistic. There is too much at stake for the Americans. (*Almost as if she is thinking aloud*) You know, if one does these things one must plan in advance and prepare for all eventualities. Operation Baghdad is a non-starter. Impossible plan.

DEFENCE MINISTER. But something has to be done, Madame! We can't ignore the provocations.

PM (*nodding*). True. There is a more risky, but also a

more attractive way. (*They look at her. Pause.*) The
Falklands option. (*Both men are puzzled*) It's clear
enough. We are a democracy. We are all elected
leaders. They are military dictators. They could
launch a pre-emptive strike any day. We pre-empt
their pre-emptive strike. (*Excitedly moves to the giant
wall map of the region*) We launch a two-pronged
attack and bomb their reactor. The regime is
unpopular. There will even be people in their
minority provinces who will greet us as liberators.
We get rid of their nuclear business, topple the
dictator, discredit their army and withdraw. A civilian government is elected. People we can talk to
seriously.

The Ministers are stunned.

FOREIGN SECRETARY. We could never get away with it,
Madame. Could we?

She smiles.

DEFENCE MINISTER. A full-scale war? The Army—

PM. Is there to fight. We spend enough on it, don't we?
(*Smiles*) Don't look so worried. We will succeed. No
one else knows as yet. So if the Americans call on
me tomorrow, I'll know it's one of you. (*Laughs as
they look shocked and then smile.*)

DEFENCE MINISTER. There is one problem, Madame.

Unless this Golden Temple business is sorted out, we will be obstructed. We can't go to war with our border province in turmoil.

PM. First we'll clear up the temple. Then we'll clean up next door.

Scene 20

EXTERIOR. STATE DEPARTMENT BUILDING, WASHINGTON, DC.

A large limousine draws up outside the building. Chuck and a senior CIA officer, Kurt, get out and slowly ascend the stairs. We see them walking in.

Scene 21

INTERIOR. STATE DEPARTMENT BUILDING.

Chuck and Kurt walk towards the lift. As they wait . . .

KURT. You've gotta keep very, very cool Chuck. I'll do all the talking. If I need you, I'll signal.

Chuck smiles and nods. They enter the lift with the others. We follow them in as they go up.

Scene 22

INTERIOR. OFFICE OF HEAD OF SOUTH ASIA DESK. STATE
DEPARTMENT.

*The room is functional. A large map of South Asia on the
wall. Portraits of JFK and Adlai Stevenson are prominently
displayed. The white-haired man at the desk is Arthur
Nelson. He is deep in conversation with a veteran American
journalist, Bigart Walsh.*

NELSON. Don't get me wrong, Biggy. I know what she's
capable of, but you've just returned from the
region. She tells us that there are training camps
set up just near her borders and we're involved
with them. True or false?

WALSH. True. I was proudly shown two of them by an
old acquaintance in Inter-Services Intelligence.

NELSON. So she's right, goddammit. (*Walsh nods*) No
one in this city's prepared to admit we're involved.

WALSH (*laughing cynically*). Very little happens in that
country without our involvement.

NELSON. Now Biggy, hold on. We are NOT involved in
their clandestine nuclear project.

WALSH. Yet! A bit difficult given we toppled their only
elected leader because he refused to toe the line

on the bomb. But we will be, soon. (*Smiles.*)

The phone rings.

NELSON (*lifts receiver*). Yeah. Give me half a second and
send them in. (*Hanging up*) Clear off, Biggy. The
big boys're here. If they see you, they might withdraw my security clearance. (*Walsh rises*) And Biggy,
this was all off the record. I do not wish to read it
in the *Times* tomorrow or the day after. At least not
just yet. (*Walsh leaves. Nelson pretends to be engrossed
in a file as there is a knock on the door.*) Enter, enter!
(*Kurt and Chuck walk in. Kurt is all smiles as is Nelson.
They both shake hands cordially.*) Welcome. I see
you've brought your Young Turk with you. Hi
there, Chuck. (*Shakes hands*) Old Kurt and his
Young Turk! (*Laughs. The other two smile. All sit. To
Chuck*) Now young man, I've heard your story. It's
preposterous. Operation Baghdad is a chapter
from the *Arabian Nights*. Pure fantasy.

KURT. The evidence is all there.

NELSON. What evidence? Nonsense. It's one of their
game plans. I've read the Ambassador's report. He
agrees with her. So do I. (*Stares hard at Chuck*)
Convince me otherwise.

CHUCK (*looks at his superior, who nods*). Well Sir, the
General who gave the plan insisted it was real and
NOT a game plan. He's been our most reliable

informant in that army for years. Never been wrong, yet.

NELSON. I trust we pay him well.

CHUCK (*ignoring the remark*). He knows she's shelved it temporarily but he's convinced that something is up.

NELSON. Oh, I'm sure something's up. How could it not be when we're helping arm and train a bunch of terrorists right next door? We try and destabilize her regime and then expect her to smile and take it?! (*Shakes his head.*)

KURT. Art, I assure you that the CIA is not training Sikh terrorists.

NELSON. Maybe. Maybe. (*Smiling*) But someone is. Who?

KURT. I don't know.

NELSON (*laughs loudly*). You don't know, Kurt? But it's your job to know. What do your agents in that country tell you? After all, most of its Generals are on our side. Have you never asked them? (*Long silence*) Listen, boys. I've been at this desk for 20 years. Most of their complaints against us are justified. It's the only motherfucking democracy in the Third World. Kennedy understood that fact well. He sent Galbraith as Ambassador. Relations soared. Now we're back to square one. Anyone who

doesn't agree with us . . . isn't totally in our pocket
. . . is a stinking Soviet agent. Right, Kurt?

Chuck is getting angry but controls himself.

KURT. Art, we're heavily involved in defending our
freedom in Afghanistan. That's more important
than any of your philosophical thoughts on
democracy. We've come to ask you to use your
influence and ensure that the relevant
Congressional Committee warns them publicly
that no section of America will tolerate a pre-
emptive strike against a friendly regime helping us
to fight for Afghan freedom. Art, your own former
Secretary of State described her as 'ruthless and
cold-blooded'.

NELSON. Dear old Henry Kissinger. He sure knew ruthless and cold-blooded people. General Pinochet,
for example. You sure he wasn't looking into the
mirror when he said that, Kurt? Chuck, I'm sorry. I
will not recommend any such statement from a
Congressional Committee. No!

KURT. We'll have to go to the White House.

NELSON (*smiling*). I'm surprised you haven't been there
already. (*Rises.*)

They follow suit. Handshakes all round. Fade.

Scene 23

INTERIOR. A BARE ROOM. PM'S RESIDENCE.

PM—dressed in tiny shorts and a T-shirt—is sitting on a floor-mat in the lotus position. Opposite her sits a large man—virtually nude, except for a tiny loincloth covering his genitals—her yoga teacher. The yoga is conducted in silence though there is a slight hint of intimacy as he helps her into new positions. Her body language is responsive. He is helping her by stretching her legs when there is a knock on the door. Both leap apart instinctively as if they were engaged in sex rather than in yoga. He moves to his earlier position opposite her and both sit in lotus positions in silence. There is another knock on the door. She looks up angrily.

PM (*the spell is broken*). Who is it? Come in, come in!

Her daughter-in-law enters and rushes straight to her.

DAUGHTER-IN-LAW (*whispering*). There is a very urgent message from the Foreign Office. (*PM nods wearily and dismisses her instructor with a glance. He joins both hands together and leaves, ultra-respectful.*) I'm sorry to disturb you, Ma.

PM. We were nearly finished. Where's the Foreign Office?

DAUGHTER-IN-LAW. On the phone.

PM rises, drinks a glass of water and both women leave the room.

Scene 24

INTERIOR. ROOM IN FOREIGN OFFICE.

A Foreign Office man is sitting behind a desk, clutching a phone. In front of him is a sheaf of telegrams. The clock on the wall shows the time—6.30 in the morning.

FOREIGN OFFICE MAN. Good morning, Madame. Please excuse me. I'm very sorry to disturb you but it was urgent. The Embassy in Washington has sent a message. Should I read it? Of course, Madame . . . A US Congressional Committee on Foreign Affairs has expressed concern at our Army's border manoeuvres. They claim they're worried we'll invade the neighbouring regime. Warn that consequences could be serious. Please advise on our reaction. No, no. That's all, Madame. (*Long pause*) Yes, Madame. Is that all? (*Scribbles down a message*) OK, Madame. Thank you. (*We hear the click. He writes and speaks the message.*) No basis in mischievous reports. Routine manoeuvres. Deny strongly.

Scene 25

EXTERIOR. OPEN VERANDAH. PM'S RESIDENCE.

PM in dressing gown is having breakfast with her grandchildren and daughter-in-law. She is flicking through a pile of papers while eating her toast and the children are giggling at her expressions as she discards one daily after another. Most of them are uniformly hostile. She is clearly preoccupied with the news from Washington and is not in a very social mood. The children, realizing this, consume their breakfast and are leaving when she looks up and beckons to them. She hugs and kisses both of them and they run off into the garden and out of view.

DAUGHTER-IN-LAW. Is it anything serious? You look upset.

PM (*smiling*). Nothing too serious. The Americans are up to something. I know it. (*Gets up*) I won't be back for lunch today. So don't wait . . . (*Smiles absentmindedly and walks into the house.*)

Scene 26

EXTERIOR. TRAINING CAMP IN NEIGHBOURING COUNTRY.

Two men—a white adviser and a clean-shaven Sikh officer of middle-class origin—are walking up and down in the courtyard. The trainees are taking a break.

WHITE ADVISER. The time is not important. I think a minimum of two months would be sufficient.

SIKH OFFICER. Two months, Colonel!? These men don't even speak English.

WHITE ADVISER (*smiling*). That's not a big problem. They're not being sent to an English-speaking country.

SIKH OFFICER (*totally puzzled*). Where, then?

WHITE ADVISER. That's what I wanted your advice about. There are two choices—Nicaragua and Angola (*Sikh is stunned*) Oh, surely we told you?! They've got to experience real combat! There's no other way, these days. Fire real bullets, blow up real bridges and face the enemy. So, your choice of language is Spanish or Portuguese. (*Smiles.*)

SIKH OFFICER. Is it really necessary? Why so far away?

WHITE ADVISER. Would you prefer Afghanistan?

SIKH OFFICER (*loudly*). No! (*White Adviser chuckles. Pause as they continue walking.*) If they're caught in Nicaragua, the publicity would damage our cause.

Angola's more secret, isn't it? (*White Adviser nods*)
Do you want me to tell them?

WHITE ADVISER. Yeah, sure. And explain why. They leave
tomorrow.

Sikh Officer walks to a corner of the courtyard where several
young Sikhs are waiting. They smile and nod warmly to him.
He sits with them on the floor and talks softly in Punjabi.

SIKH OFFICER (*subtitle*). All of you are going for real
training tomorrow to Africa. Long way away I
know, but the only place for real fighting. The
Hindu government we are fighting against is helping the Angolans with aid. Their friends are our
enemies. Correct?

Young Sikhs nod. One of them asks a question.

YOUNG SIKH (*subtitle*). I am prepared to die for our
cause any time, but why should I die in Africa?

SIKH OFFICER (*subtitle*). You fool! You have to live. Not
die either in Africa or here. Real combat training
is essential for your survival.

They carry on talking in low voices and the anxiety on their
faces gives way to excitement at the thought of the unknown.
Sikh Officer gets up and walks slowly to the other end of the
courtyard where White Adviser is waiting. He walks close to
him. White Adviser raises his eyes in a question. Sikh Officer
nods. White Adviser, delighted, literally pats him on the
shoulder. Sikh Officer smiles. Fade.

Scene 27

EXTERIOR. STREETS LEADING TO MILITARY GHQ.

PM's car is part of the traffic, with no special escort. Her Sikh guard sits next to the driver. We track the car as it drives to Army GHQ. The guard jumps out and opens the door. General Singh, standing on top of the steps, rushes down and greets her. Her face is tense and drawn. We see them going into the building.

Scene 28

INTERIOR. SMALL ROOM. MILITARY GHQ.

PM sits at the top of the table with three Generals around it. On the wall is a big map of the Golden Temple with arrows marked and Operation Bluestar written on top.

PM. Is there no other way, General Singh?

GENERAL SINGH. Madame, I am a Sikh. I have searched hard for another solution. We could lay siege and starve them out, but . . . but it could then arouse a new movement—we might find ourselves besieged by Sikh peasants rushing to the city to protect their temple rather than defend the terrorists.

PM *(her tone and visage changing)*. I agree. We've talked about this for three months. No other way. Let us strike quickly. *(Looks at them)* Within 48 hours?

Generals nod.

GENERAL SINGH. Madame, has Cabinet approved the plan?

PM. It will. I don't want to ruin the element of surprise. *(Smiles, and the rest laugh to break the tension)* General Singh, one more thing. Will the Sikh jawans remain loyal?

Generals look at each other. It is obviously something that has been worrying them.

GENERAL SINGH. We hope so, Madame. That is why we have to try and restrict the damage to the temple. It is a bit unpredictable.

PM. There is a precedent. When some dissident Muslims occupied the holy shrine of Mecca, the Saudi King, the guardian of those shrines, called in French commandos to flush them out. We are at least using our own soldiers commanded by a Sikh General. Hmm. You look unconvinced. (*Opens a file, takes out a single sheet of typed paper—the order of the day for the High Command. There is silence as she reads it, then stares at them. Slowly, she takes out her fountain pen from her handbag and signs the order. The silence is not broken. She rises. Generals follow suit. She shakes hands with all of them. She is about to walk out when she stops and turns round.*) General Singh, I do not envy you this task. It is always painful to do this in one's own country. I know the risks you take. I hope it goes smoothly with as little bloodshed as possible. Thank you, Generals. (*Spontaneously, the three men salute her. A flicker of a smile crosses her face as she nods and walks out.*)

Scene 29

INTERIOR. US EMBASSY.

Chuck is running down the corridors to the message room with a piece of paper in his hand. He bursts in. A uniformed sergeant is at the machine.

CHUCK. Top security code! To Washington, immediately! Attention: National Security Council. (*Sergeant nods but carries on with his work*) Sergeant! Drop EVERY-THING else and send this NOW!

Sergeant, slightly shaken, nods and takes the piece of paper from Chuck who stares angrily at him and storms out.

Scene 30

INTERIOR. SITTING ROOM. PM'S RESIDENCE.

*PM walks into the room, her shoulders hunched, her face
drained of energy. Dishevelled. Almost limping. She sits down
in an armchair and a servant enters quietly, followed by PA.
The servant puts a tray with tea and sandwiches on the table
and exits. PA remains standing in the corner of the room near
the door. She has not noticed him—the decision she has just
taken is weighing her down. PA coughs discreetly. She looks up
at him. He moves forward, pours her a cup of tea and hands it
to her. She sips and her mood begins to change.*

PM. Who is it now?

PA. Madame, it's the famous poetess from the land of
  the Generals. She has been waiting for an hour
  already.

PM nods and rises, consuming a sandwich.

PM. Even though she lives in Paris, she knows more
  about the Generals than our Intelligence. I'll see
  her. Now.

*We track PM out of the room and the house, crossing over to
the offices next door where she often meets visitors. As she
walks down the path, her guards, including the Sikh who
accompanies her and another, stand at attention. She smiles
and walks through the tiny gate to her offices.*

Scene 31

INTERIOR. WHITE HOUSE BASEMENT. WASHINGTON, DC.

A meeting of the National Security Council is in progress.

UNIFORMED OFFICER. We received information a few
    hours ago. The Indians have decided to capture
    the Golden Temple by force. Their army units are
    on standby.

CIVILIAN. So what? It's their business. We're not
    involved in this one. Are we?

UNIFORMED OFFICER. No sir, but we are involved next
    door. If she's successful here, she might go for
    Operation Baghdad.

CIVILIAN. She might anyway. The temple will be a mess.
    Operation Baghdad could distract attention, but
    that's pure speculation. No proof. None at all.
    (*Lots of nods around the table*) Next business.

Scene 32

INTERIOR. TRAINING CAMP.

A small shack. White Adviser and Sikh Officer, sipping whisky or something similar from a flask. Sikh Officer is agitated.

WHITE ADVISER. I can't let you go. Too dangerous. What can you do anyway except get killed? The army'll capture the temple. Yeah sure, they'll kill the priest and his friends. You must think of what'll happen afterwards. The temple is lost but the real battle's yet to come. You see that, don't you?

SIKH OFFICER *(desperately)*. But Colonel Grogan! *(The American frowns at the use of his name)* Sorry. I'm sorry. Three of my closest friends are in the temple.

WHITE ADVISER. I'm sorry. I lost my best friends in Nam. Even if I were to let you go now, you'd never get near the temple. It's been surrounded by now.

Scene 33

EXTERIOR. LAWN OUTSIDE PM'S OFFICE.

PM is chatting to exiled poetess. Her mood is now relaxed and friendly, like an aunt rather than a tough leader.

PM. Now it's my turn to ask questions. I've read your book. You seem to know the way these Generals function. Do you think they're on the verge of unleashing a war against us? You do know we've received reports suggesting a plot to try and secure their own power base?

POETESS (*surprised*). I don't think they will. That would be suicide and no ruling group commits suicide voluntarily. To invade you could only be a death wish!

PM. How can you be so sure, my dear?

POETESS. Madame, I loathe the dictator. Loathe him with all my heart. The regime regards me as a public enemy—I am not allowed back into the country and my poetry is banned. I have no time for them. I even wish they would invade you. It would be the end for them. But he's not a fool. Rather the opposite. He'll never attack you. Apart from everything else, the Americans won't let him. He can't fight a war on two fronts. Afghanistan is bad enough without taking you on. On this I insist. It's impossible.

PM (*smiling*). You know, I'm amazed how someone like
you totally ignores the dimension of irrationality.
These Generals are all the same—one-dimensional
creatures. After we won the war in 1971, they wanted
to carry on. They rushed in to see me. 'Madame, we
can finish them off. Please don't agree to a ceasefire!'
The fire was in their eyes. I told them to calm down,
reminded them that in our country the Cabinet took
these decisions. The same day I convened a special
Cabinet meeting. Most of them were for more blood.
But when I'd finished, I had a unanimous Cabinet.
Then I instructed the Generals to order a ceasefire
and not invade West Pakistan. They were fuming,
but they saluted and carried out their orders. I'm
not sure that could happen even in the United
States. (*Chuckles*) But the Generals next door are a
law unto themselves. No civilian restraints. And you
treat them as rational men!

POETESS. There is a difference between irrationality
and suicide.

PM. We shall disagree. How are your parents? Still in
Lahore? (*Poetess nods*) Give them my regards. I
wonder if I'll ever see Lahore again. We used to
stay at Aikman Road in the old days. (*Rises, as does
Poetess, and shakes hands.*)

Poetess is escorted out by a liveried servant.

Scene 34

INTERIOR. RECEPTION AT US EMBASSY.

Ambassador and wife—dressed formally—are entertaining dignitaries at a cocktail party. General Lal is present with medals pinned to his evening dress. He is joking with Chuck. A junior Embassy person comes and whispers in Chuck's ear. He exchanges glances with General Lal, looks at his watch and rushes to Ambassador. Draws him aside and whispers.

AMBASSADOR *(clapping his hands)*. Ladies and gents. Sorry to interrupt you but I have been informed that the Prime Minister is due to give a special broadcast to the nation on radio and TV in a few minutes. I'm sure you're all interested.

Murmurings and exclamations as everyone moves towards Ambassador. A TV is wheeled in and switched on.

TV ANNOUNCER *(voiceover)*. We are interrupting all our programmes for a special broadcast by the Prime Minister. *(Paper is handed to him)* I'm sorry, but the broadcast has been delayed. The Prime Minister will speak to you in . . . er . . . er . . . about half an hour.

Pandemonium breaks out and some guests rush off, including General Lal.

Scene 35

INTERIOR. ROOM IN TV CENTRE.

PM is sitting at a table and going through the script with a pencil. She is flanked by two Cabinet Ministers (Home and Defence) who are standing silently and respectfully, watching her. As far as she is concerned they could be peons. Her PA is standing near the door.

PM (*irritated*). The tone is vital. We cannot antagonize every Sikh in the country. (*Scribbling away*) We have to offer the moderates something . . .

Scene 36

US AMBASSADOR'S RESIDENCE.

The first thing we see is PM on the TV screen and it is not until later that we realize where we are. She is in a maroon sari. Her tone is more sorrowful than angry.

PM (*on TV*). Even at this late hour, I appeal to the Akali leaders, who I know are moderate men, to call off their threatened agitation and accept the framework of the peaceful settlement we have offered. The real problem is not the Akali leaders, but the fact that they have allowed the Golden Temple to be taken over by extremists and terrorists of the worst order. The reality that has emerged is not the adequacy of the settlement we are offering but the fact that the agitation is now in the hands of those who (*icy and hard*) have scant regard for the unity and integrity of our country. The occupation of the temple and the breakdown of law and order is uppermost in all our minds. The whole country is deeply concerned. An impression has been created . . . assiduously created . . . that we are not dealing with it. Let us join hands to heal the wounds. I appeal to everyone in the Punjab: don't shed blood, shed hatred . . .

AMBASSADOR. Well that's that. Now for the fireworks.

TV ANNOUNCER. We have some more news from Punjab. The Governor has called in the Army to aid civil authority. A curfew has been imposed in Amritsar as of now.

Archive footage of soldiers surrounding the Golden Temple.

CHUCK. If she pulls this one off, there'll be more trouble.

UNIDENTIFIED INDIAN (*in an ultra-British accent*). Dear me, no. How wrong you are. If this proves to be a blunder, then your lot next door had better watch out. (*Laughs and downs his drink.*)

Ambassador and Chuck exchange glances as the party breaks up.

Scene 37

INTERIOR. FIELD COMMANDER'S HQ.

GENERAL SINGH (*on the phone*). Madame, we are about to
commence operations. Yes. Yes, Madame. Please
don't worry. We have an order of the day which is
to minimize casualties. Yes.

Scene 38

INTERIOR. BEDROOM. PM'S RESIDENCE.

PM pacing up and down in her night clothes. Waiting for the phone to ring. As she lies on the bed, the phone rings. It is almost dawn. She lifts the receiver and her voice sounds as drained as her face.

PM. Yes. How many casualties? Hmm. Is it all over? It was a difficult operation, General. Congratulations. (*Sinks back into bed and drinks a glass of water.*)

Scene 39

EXTERIOR. TRAINING CAMP.

A week after the attack on the Golden Temple. Five young Sikhs, their faces, clothes and hair full of dust, are being driven into the compound. The day's activities are over and some of the trainees are sitting outside, chatting. As the jeep enters the compound, all of them rush to greet the new arrivals. Sikh Officer embraces every new man and we see tears pouring down their faces. Others bring them sherbet and glasses. The newly arrived Sikhs go to the tap in the corner and silently wash their faces. From a distance, White Adviser and a local Colonel are viewing the scene.

SIKH OFFICER (*subtitle*). Come inside. There is food.

They all go into what passes for an army mess but is actually no more than a makeshift shack with a tin roof and mud walls. Close-up on the two who have been watching all this from afar.

WHITE ADVISER. All these chickens will soon be going home to roost. The Golden Temple business was botched from beginning to end. (*Chuckles*) Makes my job easier.

LOCAL COLONEL. What exactly is your mission? I know you're helping train these guys, but is that all?

WHITE ADVISER. Sure! It's what they're paying me to do.

LOCAL COLONEL. And after you've finished here?

WHITE ADVISER. Back to Honduras. Training Contras. If only they were half as dedicated as these guys.

LOCAL COLONEL. You know, I'd never be able to fight for any other country but my own. (*Adviser chuckles*) You think I'm old-fashioned?

WHITE ADVISER. No, no, Just naïve. Whaddya think I'm doing here? (*Laughs*) The world is a small place, you know. (*Slight pause*) By the way Colonel, how many of your officers and men are leased to the Saudis and the Gulf states? About a quarter of your army, isn't it?

LOCAL COLONEL. No, no, not that much . . . (*Stops and stares at Adviser who is laughing again*) Oh, I see what you mean. Well, our excuse is that we're defending Islam.

WHITE ADVISER. You defend your type of Islam. We defend our sort of freedom.

Sikh Officer has been walking towards them from the direction of the mess in a rather agitated way. He now joins them.

SIKH OFFICER. The boys were in the temple. They say it was a bloody massacre.

WHITE ADVISER. Your holy man wanted to be a martyr. He is one. He knew it would help the cause.

SIKH OFFICER. And there've been mutinies in the Indian Army. At least a dozen Sikh soldiers have demonstrated their feelings. Hundreds have been arrested. There might be court-martials.

WHITE ADVISER. Sure, and they'll be presided over by Sikh officers. You know, like the Sikh General who led the attack. And the mutinies were a short-lived affair. All they did was to alert the High Command. Security is now very, very tough. And we have our own work to do. The new boys can't be taken to Angola yet. They'll have to train here.

LOCAL COLONEL. The General is coming here on inspection next week. Better put on something good. Or else I'm in trouble.

All smile.

Scene 40

INTERIOR. CABINET ROOM.

A Cabinet meeting is in progress. Fifteen ministers are seated around a table. The PM presides.

HOME MINISTER. . . . I would say that, despite everything, the operation was a success. The occupation of the temple is over and—

DEFENCE MINISTER (*interrupting*). And it wouldn't have been possible in the first place if wrong advice had not been given to us. The Army High Command is unhappy because of the mutinies and it will take us at least a year to stabilize the situation.

PM. There would never have been any trouble in the Army if the men had been properly briefed. They should have been told that our aim was to restore the temple as a place of worship. They should have been shown photographs and films of those terrorists in the temple and been informed as to why the action was necessary. The Army High Command failed to do that and paid the price. I do not believe that we need a year to recover. (*Looking angrily at Defence Minister*) Are you telling me that if our country is attacked, we will not be able to defend ourselves?

DEFENCE MINISTER. No, no, no, Madame! I was thinking more about the internal situation.

PM. Hmm. Is there anything else on the agenda?

HOME MINISTER. Madame, we have to tighten security arrangements. Particularly for you, but also for all members of the Cabinet. Intelligence reports are coming in and some of these fanatics have pledged to kill us all. Their publications in England . . . you know in Southall, Madame . . . are very violent in tone. So I hope all of you will accept more stringent security precautions.

PM (*nods impatiently*). Of course, of course. Do what you want, but I will not stop addressing mass meetings. No. Not even for a day. That's if you want to win the next general election. (*All smile. She rises and everyone tries to rise before her. All Ministers troop out except Defence Minister. Both of them are standing and she is deep in thought. He is waiting for her to speak. She lets him wait. Then she signals to him with a nod of her head and he follows her out of the room. We track her down the corridor. Not a word is said as both of them go down the stairs and out to the front where her car is waiting. The security is much greater and there are jeeps with armed police both in front of and behind her car. We see the car driving away from South Block through the streets.*)

Scene 41

INTERIOR. PM'S CAR.

She is silent for a while. Then in a very gentle voice, and very causally, she begins to speak.

PM. What did you mean about needing a year to recover?

DEFENCE MINISTER (*realizing he cannot deceive her*).
Madame, if we were to embark on what you called the Falklands option there might be problems.

PM (*her voice changes suddenly and pierces the atmosphere like a thunderblast*). WHY?

DEFENCE MINISTER. To go for that option with our most prosperous border province disaffected and er . . . er . . . they are training Sikhs to fight against us in such an eventuality. And . . . er . . . I am worried, Madame, That's all.

Car has reached its destination which is the military GHQ, but she dismisses the chauffeur and the guard (not the familiar Sikh this time). Both men wait outside. We can see the uniforms hovering in the background.

PM (*very sharply*). Don't you understand anything? The Falklands option would help solve several problems simultaneously. External and internal. The majority of Sikhs are patriots. They will always fight for India. To think otherwise is to accept terrorist propaganda. That is our position. Have I made myself clear? (*He nods helplessly*) You are meant to represent the interests of the country as a whole. Not . . . I repeat NOT just those of the Army.

DEFENCE MINISTER (*surrendering totally*). Of course, Madame. Please don't misunderstand . . . (*She nods to the guard who opens the door. She smiles and is greeted by uniforms.*)

Defence Minister follows. We see them entering the military building.

Scene 42

EXTERIOR. TRAINING CAMP.

*Sikh Officer is inspecting the eight Sikhs being sent to Angola
for training in real combat, now neatly dressed in civilian
clothes. From a distance, Colonel, White Adviser and a
General are watching the tableau.*

SIKH OFFICER (*softly*). No need to worry about anything.
We've cleared everything with the British authori-
ties. You will remain in transit in London. Don't be
tempted to leave the airport. I know Southall is
close by, but we have no clearance for that . . . At
London, you will be met and accompanied by a
contact to West Indies. From there, you will be
taken in a special plane to the training zone.
Everything will be all right. OK?

*Their faces are tense and worried but they nod and he shakes
hands with all of them and embraces each in turn.*

GENERAL (*to White Adviser*). We agreed to set up this
camp for our own reasons. I'm not sure about this
Angola jaunt. These johnnies will find Africa very
frightening. Everything's different there.

WHITE ADVISER. General, do you or do you not want
these men trained efficiently? You want them to

fight on your side if there is another war, don't you? (*General nods*) Then there is no substitute for real combat. You wanna know why? Because it removes fear. We can't do that here . . .

General and Colonel exchange looks and smile. Then General laughs and pats White Adviser on his back. Latter just stares back with a trace of a smile. Three cars drive in at a distance and the Sikhs in civilian gear get into them. The cars drive off in a cloud of dust.

Scene 43

INTERIOR. MEETING ROOM. MILITARY GHQ.

The meeting has been going on for some time. The three Generals look exhausted as does Defence Minister. PM alone is radiant and in her element. On the wall is a large map of the region where various pins have been stuck to explain military logistics to PM. As we enter this room there is silence: everyone except PM is deep in thought. She is waiting for a reply.

PM (*with a smile*). It was a simple question. Are the greatest military commanders unable to reply?

GENERAL SINGH. Madame, with respect, it is not up to us alone. It depends on how successful our Air Force has been. If we have superiority in the air, then I do not foresee any major problems. Provided that we do not extend our supply lines too far.

PM (*laughing*). I have no plans to shake hands with the Soviet army across the Afghan frontier. What you say makes good political and military sense. Our aims are simple. We destroy their nuclear enrichment plant. We get rid of the military dictatorship and sign a peace treaty with an elected government. You see, I am convinced that this time we will find many people there, especially in Sindh, wanting us to win.

GENERAL SINGH. Madame, you have forgotten one thing. We are determined to get rid of the camps where they are training Sikh terrorists. (*Looks at another General.*)

GENERAL X. Our information is that there are at least a dozen of these camps. Two boys trained there were coming back. One of our anti-smuggling patrols grabbed them. They had nothing on them except fake British passports. They didn't look like smugglers. They were handed over to us. We questioned them for two weeks and one of them spilt the beans.

PM. When? Why wasn't I told? Did he tell you the truth or what you wanted to hear?

GENERAL X. This happened two weeks ago, Madame. The boy only talked yesterday.

A sudden silence and tension in the room.

PM (*grim*). What did he say?

GENERAL X. He gave us the location of one camp, which ties in with other reports. He said that they were coming back to guide another 20 boys over there. Gave us their addresses. We've picked them up. They were waiting. He said that they were being trained in ordinary combat in his camp. Nothing very specialist. (*She frowns*) Their operation is very clear. They want a fifth column to disrupt us from within. I'm sure they'll dress these boys up in our uniforms and say they mutinied and joined them. So it's both practical and useful propaganda. He said something else, but I don't really believe it. (*Pause*) He said that some of them were being sent to somewhere in southern Africa . . . he couldn't remember where . . . for real combat training.

PM. Were there any Westerners in the camp?

GENERAL X. He saw one man, but they never spoke to him directly.

All of them take in this information.

GENERAL SINGH. We knew something was going on, but this is the most detailed information we've received, Madame.

PM (*in a sudden burst of anger*). And are there still doubts about what needs to be done? Well? Are there?

GENERAL SINGH. There were never doubts about the project, Madame. Only the timing, but I think we will be ready by the end of November. (*She nods approval and looks as if she is ready to end the meeting*) One more thing, Madame. Was there any particular reason why you didn't grant General Lal's extension? He was widely respected and we could have used him for this operation.

PM (*cold and brutal*). Are you absolutely sure of that?

GENERAL SINGH (*nervous and looks to other Generals for support. They remain silent*). I . . . er . . . er . . . think so, Madame. He was excellent in 1971 and—

PM (*interrupting him first with a look*). It is true. He was widely respected. Especially in Washington. He's been a CIA man for 15 years. (*Generals are shocked*) The Russians showed me proof. The least I could do was not to grant him an extension. (*Tone changes*) I think that's all for today. (*They nod. She rises. They jump to their feet.*) When will you have a detailed plan ready?

GENERAL SINGH. Within a week, Madame.

She smiles at him.

Scene 44

INTERIOR. A HALF-EMPTY RESTAURANT. WASHINGTON, DC.

Kurt and the retired General Lal are seated at a corner table. Kurt's bodyguard and chauffeur are seated a few tables away.

KURT. Can't you be more specific? The National Security Council likes detail. (*Laughs and pours himself another glass of wine.*)

LAL. As you can see, I'm now a respectable civilian. I have no access. No security clearance and, I'm afraid, no details. I know that one day before she was to decide whether or not to extend my service, the Head of KGB at the Soviet Embassy called on her with their Ambassador. I don't know, but I'm sure it was to do with me. The very next day they told me that since I was due to retire in three weeks all my clearances had been suspended. It's a routine security measure which I had put into effect at the time of our border war with China.

KURT (*ignoring much of this and apparently more involved with his food*). In that case, how do you know anything? You told us about Operation Baghdad. We backed your hunch. Now it appears what she told our Ambassador was correct. It was a game plan.

LAL (*agitated*). Sir, I beg to submit that it was NOT. She decided she wanted something more. I know something is being planned because an old friend in the Air Force told me last week. They are shifting planes like mad, but at night. During the day, it seems our fighters are still where they were but they are dummies. I give you my solemn oath that she's planning an attack this autumn.

KURT. Where's your evidence?

LAL (*tense, edgy, embarrassed*). I've been having a fling with the wife of a senior colleague. It's gone on for 10 years. (*Kurt is now on full alert*) She told me two weeks ago that her husband had returned from a top-level meeting with *her*. He could talk of nothing but her determination and her leadership qualities. His wife . . . my friend . . . got interested. He told her that they were planning big fireworks next door and went on repeating 'she's right as usual'. He's been on border manoeuvres ever since.

KURT. You know her well. When will she strike?

LAL. November. Maybe even December. You see, there'll be snow in Kashmir and that'll make it difficult for the other side to try an attack. It'll be a two-pronged attack on Punjab and Sindh. (*Kurt stares at him*) I'm prepared to pledge my life on this . . .

KURT. Might take you up on that . . . You've got a farm in California, haven't you?

LAL (*nodding and smiling*). And what if I'm right and you don't act on the information?

KURT (*guffawing*). Heads will roll. Heads will roll. 'Bring us the head of Kurt Anderson,' they'll say . . . and I might have to hide in an ashram in the Himalayas!

Both laugh.

Scene 45

EXTERIOR. LAWN. PM'S RESIDENCE.

It is a late afternoon in early autumn. PM is having tea with her family. Her grandchildren are listening, entranced, to her stories.

PM (*eating a biscuit*). I can't even think about that. You don't know how lucky you are. In those days we couldn't play like you do. We were always waiting for the police to arrive and arrest your great-grandfather. His clothes were always packed—

GRANDDAUGHTER. But that was nice. He wrote you all those letters. No one ever writes to us.

PM (*laughing*). You're too busy watching videos to read anything. It's just as well I'm here and not in prison.

PA approaches, smiling at the children. They frown at him, knowing he has come to take her away.

PA. Excuse me. I'm very sorry, but you agreed to see the guard for a few minutes. (*She nods.*)

PA turns and nods to a servant, who disappears and returns with Sikh Bodyguard, now out of uniform. He joins both hands in a salute and bows his head.

PM (*to Bodyguard*). What's wrong with you? You've had a long holiday. What do you want?

SIKH BODYGUARD (*dropping to the ground and touching her feet*). I've been loyal to you for many years, Madame. Now they say I can't guard you any more because I'm a Sikh. (*Weeps and looks away.*)

PM. Is that what they said? (*He nods*) And that's what you want? (*He nods again*) I'll think about it. Now get up and go. (*He looks at her gratefully and walks away. She looks at PA.*) Tell them to reinstate him. We can't punish every Sikh for the crimes of a handful of terrorists. Put him back on duty.

PA nods and takes his leave.

GRANDDAUGHTER. But Daddy said he didn't like the look of him after the temple was raided! He said he felt a chill when the man stared at him!

PM (*laughs*) Nonsense. What nonsense! For all his love of computers, your father's too superstitious. (*Laughs. In the distance, a stoutish figure of a woman in her early sixties, attired in a beautiful sari and carrying an exquisite shawl, is waddling over slowly to the party. PM waves at her*) Now off with you. (*Children groan, get up and walk away passing the smart lady on the way. She pats their cheeks. They smile politely.*) You're late.

SMART LADY (*sinking into the sofa*). I've been at the American Embassy, planning the Festival of India. They want it in November. (*PM stiffens slightly*) I said, fine. They asked, 'Could you check if it's OK with the PM?' They want you there to open it all. I promised to let them know tomorrow.

PM. Fine. Fine. As long as it's only for a few days. Tell them yes. What else?

SMART LADY. Everyone's gossiping about RK's new girl-friend. She's only 19. Used to be a model in Paris. Everyone knows but his wife (*PM smiles*) and you'll never guess who Younis' been eyeing.

PM giggles in anticipation.

Scene 46

INTERIOR. WHITE HOUSE. WASHINGTON, DC.

A meeting has been going on for some time. In addition to all the faces present last time, we see Kurt Anderson of the CIA.

CHAIR. Gentleman, I know we're exhausted. Some of you were opposed to this being put on the agenda again but the CIA insisted it was an emergency. You've heard Kurt here describe what is at stake if that regime collapses. Suggestions? Secretary of State?

SECRETARY OF STATE. I'm still not convinced. The State Department's experts in the field insist that it's pure speculation. They remind us of the Operation Baghdad scare and say this is more of the same. We are now at the end of September. In October, the lady's off on a speaking tour of her country which is larger than our own. In November, she's agreed to come to New York and open the Festival of India. In December, she's scheduled to visit Scandinavia and the Soviet Union with a stopover in Yugoslavia. I agree it could all be a blind, but on the face of it she doesn't look like she's preparing for war.

SECRETARY OF DEFENCE. I agree. I could add that there has been no sabre-rattling of the sort that has preceded other wars in the region. Intelligence reports no troop build-ups near the border. At least not yet. All we have is unsubstantiated speculation.

KURT (*calm, smiling*). Exactly what I thought when our contact broke the news. Then I checked a few things out with other agents in the field. Their Air Force has been placed on alert. They've moved their MIGs to very carefully camouflaged secret airfields. There is no troop build-up on the border. I agree. But they could move up in 12 hours. The space of one night, gentleman. Let me ask you something—suppose the information was confirmed? What then? (*Looks at Secretary of State who stares back silently as does Secretary for Defence. He looks at Chair.*)

CHAIR. It's obvious. She's got to be stopped at all costs. (*Others nod*) Stopped *before*. If they start a war, then it becomes very difficult to control the situation.

SECRETARY OF STATE. Hang on there. We still have no proof.

KURT. The proof is in the field of operations. We're never gonna get a document setting it all out. There might not even be such a document.

SECRETARY OF DEFENCE (*chuckles*). This is where you're wrong. Your company functions like that. Not governments. She has to give a signed order to her Generals.

KURT. Sure. She could do that at 3 a.m. on the morning when their jets slink out and blast installations across the border. We could get hold of the document then, but it would be a bit late, wouldn't it? Gentlemen, I am one hundred per cent certain that there will be a war there this fall. Unless we stop it dead in its tracks. The scale of our operation in Afghanistan alone should be sufficient not to take any risks.

CHAIR. We are agreed. If we are convinced that they mean war, we are to stop it. Is that agreed? (*All nod*) OK, that closes this meeting of the National Security Council. Could all members of the South Asia Crisis pl—

Most of the members rush away but Chair signals to Kurt to stay and an army officer in uniform stays behind as well.

KURT. Look here, Art. Our man's been screwing the wife of the General who's planning the operation. It's from the mare's mouth. All we don't have is the date. Now what?

UNIFORMED OFFICER. We've gotta act. That's for sure, but it can't be handled by the CIA or the DIA. It's gotta be a covert operation. A case for the retired General West?

CHAIR (*staring hard at CIA boss*). Kurt, you are sure, aren't you? (*Kurt nods*) Then get West.

KURT. Who'll brief the President?

They all look at each other and smile.

CHAIR. I'll report the discussions of the Council to him and tell him what was agreed. That's all. He's not very fond of the lady. Thinks she's a crypto-Commie.

KURT. West is holidaying in the Caribbean. He'll want money. People he gets to work for him will want money. Money from where?

UNIFORMED OFFICER. How much will you need?

KURT. About six million dollars. What about the Saudis?

Uniformed Officer and Chair look at each other.

UNIFORMED OFFICER. They've given enough for the Contras in return for some AWACS. (*Smiles*) Well, Sir, we did sort of agree that for special emergencies we could use some of the Contra money. I guess this is an emergency.

CHAIR. I suppose it is. OK. Take it from there. I'll authorize it. Please don't make any written reference to this. Kurt, keep all receipts so *we* know.

UNIFORMED OFFICER. And don't let West give the Generals there too much pocket money. They're making enough out of heroin already. Out of our goddammed kids.

Scene 47

EXTERIOR. TRAINING CAMP.

Early evening. White Adviser and Sikh Officer are sitting outside at a makeshift table, drinking whisky.

SIKH OFFICER. Why won't you tell me where we're going?

WHITE ADVISER. No one's told me. All I have is two clean passports and two tickets to London. At Heathrow, we'll be diverted to wherever they want us to go. Here's your passport. Better get some sleep. A helicopter's flying us to the airport in a few hours' time.

SIKH OFFICER (*looking at his British passport and shaking his head in wonderment*). You know, I tried three times over the last 10 years to get a visa to work in Britain. Refused. And now this. Is it legal?

WHITE ADVISER. Sure. That's your name and your picture. And that's a legal Home Office stamp. Sure it's legal. In the fight for freedom everything's legal.

Both men laugh.

SIKH OFFICER. Are we going to Angola? I haven't heard anything from our boys. You sure they're all right?

WHITE ADVISER. We're definitely not going to Angola.

And I have no bad news about the boys. I'm sure they're getting good training. Now, some sleep.

SIKH OFFICER. You sleep, man. I'll go say farewell to my comrades. They're a bit worried about us going off so suddenly. Only three days—you're sure of that?

Adviser nods. They get up and Sikh Officer walks briskly to another corner of the courtyard where the others are gambling with a set of dice, using stones for money. They've just finished eating.

TRAINEE SIKH (*subtitle*). Any news from Africa? (*Sikh Officer shakes his head*) Why not? (*Shrugs his shoulders*) How long're you going for?

SIKH OFFICER (*subtitle*). Three, four days. Nothing to worry about.

Scene 48

EXTERIOR. A GOLF COURSE ON A CARIBBEAN ISLAND.

The retired General West, a uniformed officer from the National Security Council and Colonel Ross are playing golf on a course overlooking the sea.

WEST (*getting ready to hit*). It's not easy. (*Hits*) But can be done. Costs will be high. You're offering no other protection, are you, Johnny? (*Ross shakes his head*) Who knows in the White House?

ROSS. General, the National Security Council decided to stop this war from happening. Peace must be preserved. At all costs, they said. At all costs! The President's National Security Adviser was present. He informed the President, who agreed. The exact mechanics were left to you. (*Pause*) And me! Every official agency has to be totally insulated. The President, Anderson at the CIA, the Pentagon. You name it. All have to be offered total deniability. I can offer you four million dollars in cash anywhere you want, but I cannot offer you any Save-Your-Arse memos from the White House or anywhere else. This will be our first and last meeting. No further communications until the operation's over.

WEST. Johnny boy! You've gone up in the world, haven't you?! (*Laughs*) I need five million.

ROSS. You have it.

They have now stopped playing golf. West is staring out to the sea, deep in thought. Ross is waiting for his final confirmation.

WEST. When is O'Neill arriving with our man?

ROSS (*looking at his watch*). In three hours. You'll meet them tomorrow. At the house. They're booked in for breakfast with you.

WEST. You conniving sonofabitch! You were pretty sure weren't you?

ROSS (*grins*). Generals like you never retire, do they? This island is a perfect cover. If you can fly men and guns out from here to Angola, you can do more. I was pretty sure.

West laughs and offers Ross his hand. Their hands clash and clasp each other. They walk back.

WEST. The other two were easier, weren't they?

ROSS. What are you talking about?

WEST (*reflective*). Much, much easier. What? Weren't you . . . ? No, probably not. I'm talking about the operations that got rid of two other prime ministers in that region. Simple. Both were handled internally. Wasn't difficult. We had key figures in both armies in our pocket. This one is tough but we'll devise a foolproof plan. Leave that to me. Where's the cash?

ROSS. Kurt suggested we use the same arrangement as before.

WEST. Fine by me. Good. That's settled. Now—are these rumours about your being a born-again whatever true, Johnny? Surely not?

ROSS (*extremely embarrassed*). Well, er . . . yeah! Both Rosie and I are practising Christians.

WEST. Sure. And God is, as always, I trust on our side for this one as well. You make sure he is . . . I was going to take you to a special nightspot. But . . .

ROSS. Hell, General! Being a Christian doesn't mean you lose the use of your prick!

WEST (*surprised, roars with laughter*). Glad to hear it. I was wrong. This born-again stuff sounds good. I'll pick you up at eight tonight. Might as well enjoy the island before you leave.

ROSS. One more thing. You are not, repeat, NOT to go to the country yourself! Kurt forbids it. Says the Russians will spot you.

WEST. For once I agree with that motherfucker but I'll visit the training camps just to smell the earth. I did set them up, you know. O'Neill was one of my boys. It's crucial I go to the region if not the country.

Scene 49

EXTERIOR. AIRPORT ON SAME CARIBBEAN ISLAND.

Early evening. A tiny airport with very limited facilities. A plane has landed. We see US Adviser O'Neill and Sikh Officer coming down the plane steps. Both are dressed in smart tropical suits and seem, for all the world, to be here on holiday. O'Neill is carrying golf clubs and Sikh Officer, a tennis racket. We track them across the runaway till they enter the terminal.

Scene 50

EXTERIOR. IN FRONT OF AIRPORT.

We see O'Neill and Sikh Officer walking out of the building to where an old American convertible with a black chauffeur is waiting. The chauffeur recognizes O'Neill and vice versa. The American smiles. Both men walk to the car, hand over their luggage and get in. Car drives out of the airport. Sikh Officer is impressed by the scenery but still tense.

O'NEILL. All the boys who went to Angola must have travelled this route. There's another secret airport from where we send supplies to the rebels.

SIKH OFFICER. Will you tell me now who we're going to meet?

O'NEILL (*laughs*). You still think it's the CIA, don't you?

SIKH OFFICER. I don't know. Don't trust the CIA. They use us like Kleenex. Then throw us away.

O'NEILL (*guffawing*). The retired General West is Chairman of the World League Against Communist Subversion. He was a serving officer in the Far East, but Carter sacked him. He organizes everything that Washington cannot admit to. I served with him in Vietnam. Tough guy. Doesn't care a shit about anything except fighting the Reds.

As the car drives on, we get a glimpse of the island just as the sun has set and darkness is on the verge of embracing land and sea.

Scene 51

INTERIOR. A SMALL BAR ON SAME CARIBBEAN ISLAND.

The room is small. The bar is large. There is an outdoor extension with dinky lights. Most of the clientele is local, downing rum. There is a live band outside and a woman is singing in the background. There are still a few empty tables. A few couples are dancing. West and Ross enter. They are the first white faces to be seen. Both men are now wearing gaudy bush-shirts. As they enter, West is recognized by many who say hello as he makes his way to an empty table. Immediately, two young women descend from the bar and join them. Drinks are ordered. At a distant table, three men watch West and his friend. We see these men in close-up: they are black, but not locals.

FIRST CUBAN (*in Spanish*). He's the one. Yes, in green. General West.

SECOND CUBAN. And the one with him? (*The first shrugs his shoulders. To third member of party*) Photograph their table from the bar. They'll blow them up big in La Habana for target practice.

Laughter. Third Cuban goes to the bar with his concealed pocket camera and, while ordering drinks, clicks away unob-trusively. As he does, we close-up on West and Ross. They are being stroked and massaged by the women. West is looking around and his eyes fasten on the Cuban table. As the third Cuban walks back with drinks—

WEST (*shouts to bartender*). Harry! C'mon here a minute, will you! (*Harry walks over. West points at the Cubans.*) Haven't seen those guys here before. Know them?

BARMAN. They're not from this island. Tourists. New York?

WEST (*as Harry walks away but within his earshot*). New York? No. Our niggers are too uppity. These boys are quiet.

While they are talking, the Cubans down their drinks and leave, waving salutes to neighbouring tables and even one to West. The two Americans settle down to the business at hand.

Scene 52

INTERIOR. PM'S OFFICE.

PM is sitting at her desk, wearing spectacles and reading a file. Her PA enters the room, waits patiently till she looks up. When she does so she removes her glasses.

PA. Madame, the Soviet Ambassador is waiting.

PM. Bring him in. At once. (*Exit PA. She hurriedly jots down a few remarks on the file. PA ushers in Soviet Ambassador. She rises, smiles and shakes hands warmly. Hands file to PA who exits with it under his arm.*) Welcome.

They move to a corner of the room and sit on the sofa and chairs.

AMBASSADOR (*in excellent English with a hint of an American accent*). Thank you, Prime Minister, for seeing me so quickly.

PM. It's always nice meeting you. You have so much information.

AMBASSADOR (*looking worried*). Madame, Moscow is worried. (*She looks at him, puzzled*) There is no concrete information, but there is something happening in Washington on India. They discussed it at their National Security Council meeting twice in the same week.

PM (*smiling*). I thought they were so obsessed with
Nicaragua that they had little time for us. That
small island worries them more than our giant
subcontinent. I met the American Ambassador last
week. Very friendly. Didn't raise any problems.
He's not intelligent enough to dissemble.

Soviet Ambassador roars with laughter.

AMBASSADOR. Can I tell you a story? (*She smiles and nods*)
In 1962, I was a young interpreter, especially for
visiting dignitaries from the United States. A top
American General was visiting us. The late lamented
Nikita Khrushchev threw a banquet in his honour
at the Kremlin. The year was 1962. While toasts
were being drunk, a message came in for Nikita
Sergeyevich. It was from our military. They had
downed an American U2 spy plane and captured
the pilot. The US had denied the existence of
these planes. Khrushchev was livid. He stood up
on the table, announced that we'd knocked down
their plane and then stared at the American
General who was still eating. 'You Americans,' he
shouted, 'are like dogs. You eat and shit in the
same place.' Then he walked out.

PM laughs loudly and genuinely.

PM. My father liked your Mr Khrushchev a lot, you
know.

AMBASSADOR. So do not be taken in by their normal
behaviour. The Cubans tell us that the CIA is
recruiting Indian citizens to fight in Angola. (*PM is
amazed*) We have a body. No identification marks.
No identity papers. Nothing. Except a bracelet.

PM. A Sikh!

AMBASSADOR. Exactly, Madame. They're not short of
mercenaries. Why do they need Sikhs? To train
them for something else? (*Removes a large envelope
from his briefcase and puts it in front of her*) The photographs of the dead man are here. Perhaps your
people can identify him. There is another photograph. Of the retired General West in a Caribbean
bar with Colonel Ross, who, as you know, works at
the White House. West is their unofficial hitman.
For Angola, Middle East, Central America, etc.

PM. Why Africa?

AMBASSADOR. Only place for real battle training.
Nicaragua is too dangerous. They could be detected
and captured. And then . . . ? In Angola, they
could pretend that they're Sikhs from South Africa.

PM. Thank you. Anything else?

AMBASSADOR. We are concerned that your security is
still too lax. You should be extra careful when you
travel abroad.

She shrugs her shoulders and smiles. Then looks at her watch. He rises. She joins him. They shake hands and she walks him to the door of her office.

PM. Please convey my regards to the First Secretary. I hope I shall meet him in Moscow this winter.

AMBASSADOR. We shall be honoured as always. (*Leaves.*)

She returns to her desk, thinks for a minute. Then lifts the phone.

PM (*on the phone*). Find General Singh. I want to see him this evening.

Scene 53

INTERIOR. NELSON'S OFFICE. STATE DEPARTMENT.

Night. Nelson and Walsh are engaged in a conversation which, judging from the cigarette butts and coffee containers, has been going on for a long time.

NELSON. Biggy, I've always trusted your judgement and respected your sources. But this sounds crazy. What can it achieve?

WALSH. You know how their minds work better than me. They will not accept that there can be a genuinely independent Third World country. No sir. It's an impossibility as far as they're concerned. So whenever the lady does something we don't like, we begin destabilizing like crazy.

NELSON. And you're sure they're going for the jackpot this time? (*Walsh nods*) How can you be sure?

WALSH. Why did Ross go and see West? Was it a social call?

NELSON. Nicaragua. West's been all over the place. Saudi Arabia—promising them AWACS if they'll give us the odd billion as a gift for freedom in Nicaragua. Even been to Brunei. Most Americans think Brunei's a Canadian beer! (*Both laugh*) So Ross going to the Caribbean tells me nothing.

WALSH. And what if I were to tell you that West's old hitman, O'Neill, is there too? With a Sikh leader. Then what would you say, Art?

NELSON. Source? C'mon, source?

WALSH. Come off it! He's a totally trustworthy figure in the army. Their army. Very worried that his country might be getting embroiled in a new subcontinental war. And he's perfectly right.

NELSON. I still don't believe it!

WALSH. What different does it make anyway? Even if you believed me there's nothing you could do. The B-movie men would lie and lie and lie on television.

WALSH. Others have lied in the past, but no one's believed them. Mr B-movie convinces them. (*Pause*) Let's go and eat, Biggy. Food.

Scene 54

EXTERIOR/INTERIOR. VERANDAH IN WEST'S CARIBBEAN
RETREAT.

*West's colonial bungalow is not lavish by LA standards but it
is still a small palace compared to the housing on the rest of
the island. (It is, in fact, the former residence of the planta-
tion owner.) West, O'Neill and Sikh Officer are seated around
a rectangular table on a verandah overlooking the sea and
situated just two steps above a lush tropical lawn. The table is
obviously used for larger gatherings. West is seated at its head
with the other two on either side of him. We can glimpse a
large map of South Asia hanging in the room behind them.
All three are dressed casually. West is staring at Sikh Officer.*

WEST (*to Sikh Officer*). You interest me. Don't think we
haven't checked you out. (*To O'Neill*) Did you know
he used to be a fucking Maoist? Like those nutty
weathermen we had to deal with in the 1970s.

O'NEILL. Yes Sir. He told us everything. I sent you a
long report on him and his antecedents.

WEST. That's where I must have read about it. Now, how
many armed men do you have at your disposal?

SIKH OFFICER. I think about several thousand, General.

WEST (*snorts*). You think . . . about several thousand.
Facts. Figures. Accuracy. Now, tell me again.

SIKH OFFICER. Our group has five thousand boys. Not all are trained but we are trying hard. Other groups are smaller. I don't know their exact numbers. Add them all up and we have a cadre of seven or eight thousand.

WEST. Any in the army?—not deserters, but serving officers and soldiers? And don't go on about former General Shagbag or whatever his name was . . . He's dead and of no use to us.

SIKH OFFICER (*getting angry but controlling himself*). Very few. In fact, none. But we have sympathizers in the police force. A few dozen in Punjab and some in the capital itself.

WEST. Small cogs. That's all you've got? Did O'Neill tell you? Two of your boys have been killed in Angola.

Looks at him hard to study his reactions. Sikh Officer rises to his feet and looks at O'Neill.

SIKH OFFICER. You knew! I asked you. You knew? Why? Why? Who is it?

Both men look at him and West does so sympathetically for the first time

WEST. I'm sorry. It was on my orders. We didn't want to demoralize the training camps. I'll give you the names. Now, who are your men in the police force in Delhi? How many? How reliable?

SIKH OFFICER (*still slightly distracted, but recovering*).
Before the raid on the Golden Temple, we had
nothing. Now we have 10 or 12 men in the police
force in Delhi. The highest ranking is a Sub-
Inspector. I'm sorry. But they are reliable. Would
do anything for the cause. Anything. (*Pauses. Deep
in thought*) I've just remembered. The last time I
visited our village, I met someone who was related
. . . by marriage, I think . . . to the Prime
Minister's chief bodyguard. (*West stiffens, trying to
remain calm. He downs a glass of juice.*) He told me
that even this guy who used to adore her is now
. . . after the temple attack . . . disaffected. (*Shrugs
his shoulders*) So, we are gaining support.

WEST (*now ultra-friendly*). This is all very useful. Very,
very useful! I have work to do with O'Neill here.
You, my friend, must return immediately. I want
you to go back to your village. Find that relative
and ask to meet the bodyguard. See what you
think. I want a report within a week (*Shouts*) John,
John! (*White factotum in shorts and T-shirt appears.
His demeanour is over-familiar and laid back.*) John,
you will show Mr Singh the island. Then drive him
to the airport. You know which one. Tell Arnold I
want him back at his base. (*Looks at his watch*)
Tonight. Best to get him to New York, I suppose.

SIKH OFFICER. General West, the man you want me to meet is now on their wanted list as well. He's in England. Someplace call Wolverhampton.

WEST. You sure of that? (*Sikh nods definitively*) Then our problems are over. John . . . regular airport. First flight to London. (*To Sikh Officer*) You'll be met by friends. We'll take care of all that. They'll give you money, accommodation and anything else you need! Stay with them. No wandering and meeting old friends. Your instructions are simple. Find this guy. Take him back to the camp.

SIKH OFFICER. He hasn't got any papers or money.

WEST (*impatiently*). London will give him everything. Whatever you need . . . OK?

Sikh Officer smiles for the first time, shakes hands warmly with O'Neill, formally with West and follows John out into the garden. We track them to the jeep which we see driving off while the following conversation is taking place.

O'NEILL. I don't even need to ask what you're up to . . . do I? It's crystal clear. Should have known . . .

WEST. What are you going on about? Grumbling as usual?

O'NEILL. You want to chop the top off the pyramid, don't you, General? That's all you want. Might as well disband the camps and send these mother-fuckers home.

West stares at him silently for a moment.

WEST. Washington does not want another war in South
Asia. It would distract from Afghanistan. If she
went in and toppled the Generals, the consequences could be serious. First in Afghanistan and
for the facilities we've been promised for the
Rapid Deployment Force. Since the Shah fell,
we're marooned in that part of the world. So we
want the status quo preserved. We act as peace-
makers blessed by Washington.

O'NEILL. Was this one of your ideas, General?

WEST. Heavens no! A blue-arsed fly from Washington
flew over a few days ago.

O'NEILL (*smiling*). Ross?

WEST. Correct. Handed me a blank cheque. Just stop
any possibility of a war out there. Do whatever's
necessary. 'Is that what the President wants?' I
asked him that. 'Would I be here otherwise?' That
was his response. So, O'Neill, I have to confess
that this was not my idea. I didn't even want to be
distracted from Central America. You know those
Commie-lovers in Congress. Trying to make us
fight the Reds with one arm tied behind our backs.
But orders are orders.

O'NEILL. I read you loud and clear, General. Ross left
you to work out the details and mechanisms.

WEST. But naturally.

O'NEILL As usual!

WEST. There's only one way to stop this tragedy. Remove the main actor, who in our case is also the director and playwright, from the scene. End of drama.

O'NEILL. Doesn't always work. How many times did we try and get Castro? Seven, General. Seven! Every single attempt a failure.

WEST. We! Did I hear you say WE!? No, it was the CIA. The dearly beloved Company fucked it up. The few missions we have been entrusted with have all been successful.

O'NEILL. OK, Sir. What do you want me to do?

WEST. Get back to the camps. Tell the Generals—Inter-Services Intelligence (*O'Neill nods*)—I want a special meeting in a fortnight's time. At the camp. I'll fly in on a private cargo plane at night. We've got to tell them the scale of the operation.

O'NEILL They'll want money . . .

WEST. I know. Promise them two million dollars. No more and, if possible, less. You look unsure.

O'NEILL. General, are you sure this is the right way? I mean if we succeed it could get more dangerous, couldn't it? If they uncover the links there will be a

war. A vicious one. Relations with us will be
harmed irreparably. And if we fail, having tried
. . . well, you know the lady. She won't be pleased.

WEST. Risks in anything we do. Not to mention doing
nothing. The phase of masterly inactivity as far as
she's concerned is over. Get your arse back there,
Private O'Neill.

*Both men laugh as if sharing a private joke from a bygone
campaign and shake hands warmly. Close-up of their faces:
adrenalin has begun to flow. Fade.*

Scene 55

INTERIOR. MEETING ROOM. MILITARY GHQ.

PM is seated around a table with four Generals and Air Marshall Singh, Chief of the Air Force, in full uniform, complete with resplendent turban. On the wall is a large map with red arrows pointing out the route of advance being planned by the Generals. We have entered the meeting room half-way through the discussions. General Singh, holding a large pointer, is walking back from the maps to resume his seat. For a moment there is complete silence. The Air Marshall twirls his moustache thoughtfully. PM is in a reflective mood.

PM. Hmm. So once again, Generals (*looking around*), you are telling me that success depends on the capacity of our Air Force to take them by surprise?

GENERAL SINGH. Madame, with great respect, that is not so. The speed of our success depends on the Air Force. That's all. I have no doubt that we will win, but if, as you have stressed yourself many times Madame, we wish to minimize casualties, then what his boys (*looking at Air Marshall*) do becomes decisive. Without air cover, their army will surrender within a fortnight.

PM. Perhaps. But you mustn't forget something else. Their army has become flabby. A quarter of their officers and jawans are loaned out to the Gulf States. Others are busy running the country. Some are getting rich on heroin. So even if we lose the element of surprise, we should be able to limit the war.

AIR MARSHALL. Since I've been informed of our plans I've discussed a strike strategy with some squadron commanders. Madame, have no doubt. We'll hit those blighters where it hurts. There are ways of avoiding their radar. A night attack on their nuclear reactor. Simultaneous bombing of bridges, airfields and railway tracks to cut off their capital from three of their largest cities. (*Getting carried away*) We shall toast you with gimlets at the Sindh Club, Madame!

All smile except PM.

GENERAL SINGH. Have you decided on a date, Madame?

PM (*nods*). Some time in November.

AIR MARSHALL. Only six weeks away. (*Whistles*) Well, we're ready to go Madame. All we need is 48 hours' notice. That's all. (*Looks triumphantly at the Generals.*)

PM (*rises to leave, but gestures that they keep seated. They ignore her and rise*). I have to return to a Cabinet meeting. Air Marshall, walk me to my car.

Air Marshall rises and accompanies her out of the room. Generals look at each other, almost sigh in relief and sit down in a more relaxed mood.

GENERAL SINGH. For a long time I thought she was bluffing. But it's real.

GENERAL X. Sir, my worry is not the Americans but the Chinese. What if they decide on a more active course to back the boys next door?

GENERAL SINGH. I've thought about it . . . PM is convinced that they will bark a great deal but not bite. She says the situation inside China is now very different. After the mess they made in Vietnam, they won't risk any more adventures. I agree with her.

The Air Marshall has re-entered the room, a gigantic grin all over his face and shaking his head as if he can't believe what he's heard.

GENERAL X. Share the joke, man!

AIR MARSHALL. You won't believe this . . . Do you know what she wanted to talk about? (*Heads shake*) The ruddy election of office-bearers in the Delhi Gymkhana Club! Her favourite boy's running for the Secretaryship . . . the Foreign Office doesn't keep him busy enough . . . and there's a campaign against him. I'm not surprised at all. Anyway, the Prime Minister wants me to get all the Air Force members of the Club to vote for her candidate.

Snorts of disbelief and laughter

GENERAL SINGH. And did you agree?

More laughter.

AIR MARSHALL. Of course I did. Otherwise she'd have the Club declare a state of Emergency and impose him anyway! (*Laughter*) Better that we elect him . . .

GENERAL SINGH. What a lady! Here we are planning a war and she's worried about some bugger losing an election in the bloody Gymkhana Club!

More laughter.

Scene 56

EXTERIOR. TRAINING CAMP.

Two uniformed Generals, Colonel, O'Neill and West (still disguised as a cargo hand of Southern Air Transport) are walking across the courtyard. O'Neill has a large folder. Sikh Officer sees them from a distance and walks over to them.

WEST. God. It's still hot. How do you bloody survive
     here?

Generals laugh politely and escort him into a room.

Scene 57

INTERIOR. MEETING ROOM. TRAINING CAMP.

A rough and ready room with a large solid table in the middle, a few wooden chairs placed around it. Colonel, West, Sikh Officer and the two Generals all take seats. West automatically sits at the head. The atmosphere is business-like: there is no display of camaraderie and a slight tension exists.

WEST (*to Sikh Officer*). Well?

Sikh Officer looks around, unsure.

GENERAL A (*to Colonel*). I think you should leave. This does not concern you.

Colonel nods, his face full of anger, and walks out. Other Generals follow him and we track them out of the room.

Scene 58

EXTERIOR. COURTYARD. TRAINING CAMP.

COLONEL. Sir, this is an insult! Being asked to leave the room with a foreigner present. It's OUR country!

GENERAL B. Yes, yes, OUR country, but this is THEIR operation. Organized by THEM, not US! Unnecessary for more of us to be involved than is useful. (*Pats him on the back*) Even the bulk of our High Command does not know. It's a purely Intelligence matter.

Scene 59

INTERIOR. MEETING ROOM. TRAINING CAMP.

On the table are several blown-up photographs of PM and Sikh Bodyguard. West has one in front of him.

WEST. And you're sure?

SIKH officer (*looking at pictures on the table*). He's sure!

WEST. Then he'll come here. Useful test.

SIKH OFFICER. I think so.

WEST. I can't stay indefinitely. Get him over within a week. Possible? (*Sikh Officer nods*) Good. Then that's settled. And we won't meet here. (*To Generals*) You can supply us with a tent and refreshments in the middle of nowhere—can't you?

GENERAL A. Of course, of course. No problem at all. We understand.

SIKH OFFICER. Then I'll leave now. (*Leaves.*)

General B re-enters the room.

WEST. Everything's been sorted out on your front, I trust?

Generals nod.

GENERAL B. I suppose there's no real chance of this backfiring, is there? (*West and O'Neill exchange a*

119

quick glance.) Very few people know. If there were repercussions, they'd have our balls for breakfast.

West laughs.

WEST. It'd be far more serious than that . . . I don't think there will be repercussions. At least not immediately. There might be in a few years' time, but by then you'll have your AWACS and missiles and no one will be able to get near you. Don't worry.

Scene 60

INTERIOR. PM'S OFFICE.

PM (*her face worried, speaking on the phone*). When? How? I see. Are they all right? You're sure? (*Looks at her watch*) I'll come. Hmm. (*Presses a bell under her desk. Within seconds the PA is in her room.*) Just a minute. (*To PA*) Get my car ready. Now. I'm going home for a few hours. (*Returns to her phone conversation*) Oh god! Anyway, at least they're not hurt. It's nervewracking! Come over—they're always pleased to see you. (*Puts phone down. Rises as PA enters room.*) No, no. I've got a public meeting.

PA. Everything's ready, Madame. Madame, are the children badly hurt?

PM (*beginning to walk to the door*). No. But the shock is awful. The traffic in this city is beyond a joke.

We track them out of her room down a corridor. At the top of the stairs she is joined by a bodyguard who is not the usual Sikh.

PM (*surprised at the new face*). Where's the other one? The one who pleaded with me to return? Where is he?

PA. His mother's seriously ill. He had to go back to his village.

She has reached the front of the building.

Scene 61

EXTERIOR. PM'S OFFICE.

PM's security has been doubled. She walks to her car, gets in. Then, preceded by jeeps full of armed men and motorcycle outriders, she drives off. We see the entourage on its way.

Scene 62

EXTERIOR. IN THE MIDDLE OF NOWHERE.

A tent on a rugged plain. O'Neill and West are waiting outside. Silence, except for noises of insects and birds. It is late afternoon. Hot. West uncorks a thermos and takes a long sip. Wipes the sweat off his face. The silence is disrupted by the sudden noise and appearance of a helicopter. It lands and Sikh Officer and PM's Bodyguard jump out. West and O'Neill look at each other. The two Sikhs walk forward. Bodyguard shakes hands with the Americans. Close-up of Bodyguard's face.

SIKH OFFICER. He's got to be back tonight. We've got three hours.

WEST. Success is already written on his face.

Close-up of Bodyguard's face. Fade.

Scene 63

INTERIOR. PM'S BEDROOM.

PM is sitting on the bed with her legs up. Her granddaughter is lying with her head on PM's lap and PM is stroking her hair. Her grandson is sitting on the floor, pretending to be nonchalant, and reading a book. On an armchair in the corner sits the fat friend. From the living room, strains of Bach can be heard—Concerto No. 7 in G Minor with Andrei Gavrilov on the piano. PM gets up and affectionately drags the granddaughter up as well.

PM. Come on everyone! A special tea is waiting!

Slowly, the small party moves out of the room. We track them through the tiny corridor and enter the living room. The music is now loud and we see an assortment of sandwiches (cucumber in white bread), pastries and Indian sweets of all sorts laid out on a table. PM turns music down a little. The children hug her.

PM (*to Friend*). They're unharmed. Just the shock. I couldn't bear it if anything happened to them.

FRIEND. Oh they're fine. Look at them. (*Children are busy eating and giggling*) It's you I'm worried about. You're tiring yourself out. This trip to Orissa—is it necessary?

PM (*nods and sips tea. A sandwich is poised on the saucer*).
Of course. Everything is prepared.

The children come and sit at her feet. Again she strokes their heads in turn.

GRANDDAUGHTER. We hardly see you these days. Too
busy for your own grandchildren!

PM laughs.

PM. I don't want any more escapades. I heard what
happened. You were egging the driver on to race
the other car . . . silly. Your great-grandfather used
to be obsessed with flying planes. (*Her eyes are
moist*) Just like your uncle. The British didn't let
him indulge his fantasies. They kept him in prison
for many years. Your uncle died. Both of you know
what you mean to me. I don't want any stupidities.
Now, should we all have a game of Scrabble?

Children yell with joy and boy disappears, returning in a second with Scrabble board, which he sets up.

FRIEND. I know I'll win again. It's getting embarrassing.

Laughter. There is a knock on the door. Servant enters, whispers in PM's ear. She nods. He exits, taking empty tea-trays with him. PA enters afterwards. Children look at him and groan.

PM (*puts a word on the board on a triple score. The word is VICTIM*). What is it?

PA. Sorry to disturb. A message from General-sahib. It's
   urgent.

*She looks apologetically at others and leaves the room. We
track her to the phone in her study. She lifts the receiver.*

PM. Put him on. Yes. No, no. that's all right. You can
   talk.

Scene 64

INTERIOR. GENERAL SINGH'S ROOM. MILITARY GHQ.

GENERAL SINGH (*on the phone*). Madame, Intelligence
has just informed us that retired American General
West has arrived next door, disguised as a cargo
hand. We don't know why or for how long. Beg
your pardon? No, Madame, no. He's the one they
use for ultra-covert operations. (*Pause*) You may be
right, but Afghanistan is an open war. Congress
has given them billions quite happily. West is in
charge of dirty work. Yes, Madame. Yes, I think it
is serious. When? Very well, Madame. We'll be
there.

Scene 65

INTERIOR. OFFICE/STUDY. PM'S RESIDENCE.

PM puts the phone down. Deep in thought, she walks back to the other room. She enters to see the trio totally immersed in the Scrabble game. To VICTIM has been added VAIN. She kisses the children.

PM. I'm sorry. You know—

GRANDCHILDREN (*together*). 'I have to go.'

PM (*smiling*) Yes. But when I'm back from Orissa we'll spend a morning together. I'll cancel a morning darshan and . . . (*She nods to them. Exchanges a smile with Friend. Leaves.*)

Scene 66

EXTERIOR. LAWN IN PRIVATE HOUSE. LAHORE.

*West and O'Neill are enjoying the cool of the evening. It is
the private residence of a US Intelligence official attached to
the Ford Foundation. West is dressed in tropical gear and
O'Neill too is smarter than usual. Behind both men is a
makeshift bar and they help themselves liberally to cocktails.*

WEST. Mission, nearly over.

O'NEILL. It was pure luck. And it isn't over yet.

WEST *(grins)*. No, nearly over. I was precise. And the
　　chances are good. The element of surprise is cru-
　　cial in an operation like this. So they know I'm
　　here. They found out. The press reports're full of
　　lurid speculation. But none of them could even
　　dream of what we've got.

*Sikh Officer, as smartly dressed as he was in the Caribbean, is
escorted by the lady of the house, a striking black American,
to where West and O'Neill are seated. Both men watch him
approach and wave. She leaves him half-way and he walks
over to them.*

O'NEILL. Hi. Drink? *(Sikh Officer shakes his head and sits
　　down.)* Well, we're waiting.

SIKH OFFICER. Everything is ready. *(His face is tense)*

From now on it's a field operation. We can only
call it off and even that would be very difficult.

WEST. No last-minute nerves? Cold feet? Eh?

SIKH OFFICER (*angry*). General West, you still do not
appreciate what ordinary Sikhs felt when the Army
attacked the Golden Temple. Revenge might heal
the wounds.

O'NEILL. And open new ones? Don't underestimate the
price you people will have to pay.

SIKH OFFICER. Everything for you is in terms of price
and payments . . .

O'NEILL. I wasn't referring to dollars, though you will
agree that we have not been parsimonious. You've
had all you wanted. You're now telling me that this
operation is being carried out for the highest
motives?

WEST. Suits me fine. I'll have our money back.

Both men laugh, but Sikh Officer is angry.

SIKH OFFICER. No, no. Please don't misunderstand.
Your motives and those of our organization are
very different, but the man you met is sacrificing
himself out of a duty to his religion.

WEST. Sure, sure. We appreciate that and we've made it
clear that his dependents will not suffer. (*Suddenly,
turns to Sikh Officer nervously*) What do you really
think the chances of success are?

SIKH OFFICER. Ninety-nine percent! And I will have a
    drink Major, if you don't mind.

*O'Neill smiles, rises and moves to the bar. Pours Sikh Officer
a large whisky and soda.*

WEST. I leave for Washington tomorrow. I'll meet the
    Ambassador before I go so that people think it was
    some semi-official visit.

O'NEILL. General, is that wise?

WEST. Embassy insists on it . . . (*Shrugs his shoulders.*)

O'NEILL. But they don't know why you're here.

WEST. Are you suggesting I tell them?

Both men look at each other in silence.

Scene 67

INTERIOR. HAROLD'S OFFICE. STATE DEPARTMENT.

HAROLD (*on the phone*). I don't care, George. I want you to ask that sonofabitch . . . er yes. No. I was refer- ring to Colonel Ross of the National Security Council. Yes, George. Let's not play games. If any- one knows why West went to South Asia, it's Ross. (*Long pause*) Ask who? (*Laughs*) You haven't a snow- ball's chance in hell. George, this is serious. If what you're saying is true, and I have not yet begun to doubt your word, then as Head of the CIA you do not know why West went there—right? I want you to find out. Because it affects our relations with the world's largest fucking democracy. It's not Commies you're dealing with now, George. Thank you. I will wait. (*Presses a button on the phone*) Yeah, get me Congressman Ray on Capitol Hill. (*Replaces receiver and walks to the map of South Asia, stares at it, then walks back and lights a cigarette as his phone rings. Lifts the receiver*) Hullo! Oh Mark, how are you this morning? You too. Well, I spent an hour with a very angry Indian Ambassador. They claim that West is training Sikh terrorists on the edges of their border. Oh, then you've heard it first hand.

Whaddyou think? Hmm. I agree. I think he's
right. Biggy, you know Bigart Walsh? He was with
the *Times*? Now he's a resident academic at
Cornell. He swears the camps exist. He's heard it
from the military over there. (*Long pause*) No. I've
asked the CIA officially to confirm or deny. I've
tried three times yesterday to speak to Ross. It
seems everything's out of bounds for us. Yup. Yup.
Sure thing. And the Foreign Relations Committee.
OK. Bye now, Mark. We'll be in touch. (*Buzzes
phone*) Could you try Colonel Ross at the White
House again, Maggie? And just keep trying every
10 minutes and leave the same message. Thanks.
(*Puts down the receiver.*)

Scene 68

EXTERIOR. LAWN IN PRIVATE HOUSE. LAHORE.

Sikh Officer has gone. Darkness has descended. A spotlight shines on the lawn. West and O'Neill are still drinking. Occasionally, they stop and try to hit the mosquitoes on their arms and face.

O'NEILL. General, one thing's been bothering me.

WEST. Go ahead.

O'NEILL. Suppose they capture him alive and he talks? Torture can be potent. Suppose they bring his wife before him and start working on her . . . then what? If he says he met us? Gives dates and hints and places? Describes you? It will be the biggest scandal since . . . since, well you know what I mean.

WEST. I was almost beginning to write you off. You've just won a reprieve. Everything's organized. The man we met will be shot dead. Ask no more. A million dollars are waiting for the guy who'll do it. Anything else on your mind?

O'NEILL (*greatly relieved*). What are my orders?

WEST. You stay here as usual. Three weeks after, you get your arse on a plane out of here. I'll meet you in Honduras.

Both men grin and down their drinks.

Scene 69

INTERIOR. OFFICE. STATE DEPARTMENT.

HAROLD (*on the phone*). Colonel Ross! This is a rare privilege. Thanks for returning my (*looks at pad in front of him*) two-hundredth call.

Scene 70

INTERIOR. OFFICE. WHITE HOUSE. WASHINGTON, DC.

ROSS. Get off my back, Hudson. We've got work to do here. You and that Congressman are becoming a nuisance. (*Pause. His face glowering*) No! I do not know why West was there. I do not know who sent him and I do not fucking care. (*Pause*) No, look we discuss every motherfucking country on the National Security Council. Why should India be exempt? Anyway, who the fuck are you working for? (*Pause and his face goes red again*) I've nothing more to say. Goodbye. (*Bangs down the receiver.*)

Scene 71

INTERIOR. HAROLD'S OFFICE. STATE DEPARTMENT.

HAROLD (*on the phone*). No. But he sure was rattled. Something's up. If you do find out, let me know. Bye for now, Mark. What? Oh, I'll be working late tonight. Lots of papers. Yeah. Bye.

Scene 72

EXTERIOR. AIRPORT AND ROADS.

Dusk. The airport in the capital is sealed off. PM's plane has landed on a heavily guarded tarmac. Her car drives up to the bottom of the stairs and she comes down. Bodyguard opens the door. She acknowledges his greeting and gets in the back with PA. With jeeps in front and behind, her car drives off.

Scene 73

INTERIOR. PM'S CAR.

Close-up of Bodyguard in front: his face is tense and nervous unlike on previous occasions.

PM (*to Bodyguard*). I heard your mother was ill. How is she now?

BODYGUARD (*stuttering*). Er . . . very well, Madame.

He does not turn round and look at her but keeps staring straight at the road. She shrugs her shoulders.

PA. Madame is tired?

She does not reply—just nods as the car drives into her house. Bodyguard opens door for her. She walks out, does not look at him and goes indoors.

Scene 74

INTERIOR. PLANNING ROOM. MILITARY GHQ.

Three Generals have just finished a meeting sorting out logistics, etc. for the offensive they are planning. They look tired but confident.

GENERAL SINGH (*suddenly sitting on the edge of the table*). What is a bit ominous is that there has been no response so far. They must know we're planning something. But there's no sign of any troop movements on their side of the border.

GENERAL B. Sir, maybe there have been no breaches in security this time.

Both men look at each other and laugh.

GENERAL A. Quick drink? At the club?

GENERAL SINGH. Nope. In the mess. Three Generals in the Club in full uniform at 8.30 p.m.!—the tongues will start wagging.

Scene 75

INTERIOR. DINING ROOM. PM'S RESIDENCE.

PM, grandchildren, daughter-in-law, fat friend and Ustinov are at dinner. Wine is being served.

USTINOV. The evenings have become lovely again. Madame, your secretary has confirmed for tomorrow morning.

PM. That's fine. I've cancelled my darshan because of these two. I'm spending the morning with them. (*Looks at children*) So you have half an hour.

USTINOV. What is a darshan?

FRIEND. An audience. The Mughal Emperors used to have a Hall of the People where they met petitioners from all over their empire. Your British (*Actor puffs himself up and assumes role of British Grandee. Children giggle. PM smiles.*) did something similar. And all our prime ministers meet ordinary people every morning.

PM (*wearily*). In my father's day, anyone could come but now the security's awful. Everyone is vetted and checked and the whole thing has lost its real meaning. Now, it's mainly party workers coming to grumble about their bosses.

Scene 76

EXTERIOR. PERIMETER OF PM'S HOUSE.

Darkness. Two figures are talking. One lights a cigarette and we see their faces: Bodyguard and another Sikh.

BODYGUARD (*subtitle*). It's done. You've got permission?

ACCOMPLICE (*subtitle*). Yes, yes. I said I had a bad stomach. Needed to go to toilet. Could I be on duty inside the compound? Agreed.

BODYGUARD (*subtitle*). Feeling OK?

ACCOMPLICE (*subtitle*). Yeah! When should we . . . ?

They hear steps.

BODYGUARD (*louder voice*; *subtitle*). Best thing for your stomach is some aniseed. I'm off to bed . . .

Armed guards pass by them. They exchange greetings.

Scene 77

INTERIOR. CHILDREN'S BEDROOM. PM'S RESIDENCE.

PM is tucking them in.

GRANDDAUGHTER. Daddy's never here either—

PM. That's my fault. I'm making him work extra hard. (*Smiles*) Now lie down. Should I tell you a story tonight?

GRANDDAUGHTER. Please. About when you were my age.

PM. I was alone a lot. So I used to pretend to be Joan of Arc—

GRANDDAUGHTER. What was the name of the actress you're always going on about?

PM. Greta Garbo?

We leave the room slowly as lights go out in the house.

Scene 78

EXTERIOR. FRONT OF PM'S RESIDENCE.

A police constable is standing with an umbrella to protect PM against the sun, already high and hot. We view them from above and see, in her office lawn a few seconds' walk away, Ustinov and his crew getting ready to film. PM emerges from front of house with PA and personal servant carrying her files. They walk towards the small gate which separates her personal quarters from the office space. She walks briskly, at the head of the entourage of four, and the umbrella-man can't keep up with her. Bodyguard, stationed at the gate as usual, opens the gate and greets her. Before she can step forward, he whips out a pistol and shoots her from less than three feet away. PM cries out and slumps to the ground. Accomplice jumps from the other side and empties his Thomson carbine in rapid-fire position. Her body is riddled with 20 bullets. Daughter-in-law rushes out barefoot from the house, stares at PM and drops to the ground. Security guards rush to the scene.

Bodyguard and Accomplice drop their weapons to the floor.

BODYGUARD. I have done what I had to do. Now you do what you have to do.

They are hit with rifle butts and dragged away. We hear a burst of machine-gun fire.